VENETA

Matt Dillon, New York 2019 brioni.com

Brioni

ROMA

TAILORING LEGENDS SINCE 1945

Rolex. An extremely fine and rare 18K gold chronograph
wristwatch with black dial and cherry logo signature
Ref. 6262, circa 1970

RARE WATCHES

Geneva, 11 November 2019

VIEWING
7-10 November
Quai des Bergues 33
1201 Genève, Switzerland

CONTACT
Sabine Kegel
skegel@christies.com
+41 (0) 22 319 17 25

CHRISTIE'S
INTERNATIONAL REAL ESTATE

NORTH AMERICA
New York
20 Rockefeller Plaza
New York
New York 10020
USA
+1 212 468 7182

Los Angeles
336 North Camden Drive
Beverly Hills
California 90210
USA
+1 310 385 2690

Palm Beach
313 1/2 Worth Avenue
Suite 4B
Palm Beach
Florida 33480
USA
+1 561 805 7327

ASIA
Hong Kong
22nd Floor
Alexandra House
18 Chater Road
Central, Hong Kong
+852 2978 6788

EUROPE
London
8 King Street
St James's
London SW1Y 6QT
UK
+44 20 7389 2522

Moscow
Romanov pereulok 2/6-13
Moscow, 125009
Russia
+7 495 937 6364

Disclaimer: Photography and material in the publication may not be reproduced in any form without the permission of Christie's International Real Estate, Inc. All properties featured in this booklet are subject to prior sale, change, or withdrawal without notice. All details featured in this booklet were correct at the time of press. Currency conversions in Christie's sale results reflect exchange rates at the time of sale. Christie's International Real Estate, Inc. believes all material and editorial to be correct, but assumes no legal responsibility for accuracy.

From the CEO
LOVE FOR SALES

Dan Conn, CEO
Christie's
International
Real Estate

The art market is booming. Last year more than $7 billion worth of art was sold by Christie's alone. If you're thinking about selling all or part of your collection, read our feature on page 58 for advice on how to go about it, plus gain insider know-how from Christie's experts.

As you'd expect, we have plenty of art in this, our Art & Style issue, from fascinating street photographers on page 66, each offering a unique view into the world around them, to an examination of how fashion houses have always looked to artists for inspiration when creating their collections (page 80).

Our featured properties this month are impressive, to say the least. Whitehall Estate, in Napa Valley (page 48), is an outstanding modern home and vineyard, designed by acclaimed architect Lewis Butler, while Tuscany's Villa La Vagnola dates back to 1750, and, fittingly for this issue, is filled with vibrant colors, finishes, and artifacts (page 74).

As ever, our Gallery, Gourmet, and Travel pages offer a curated selection of art, design, style, and architecture stories, as well as culinary homewares and our editors' picks of luxury hotels and destination restaurants.

We also present listings for more than 160 luxury properties for sale around the world from our exclusive affiliates, starting on page 89, while christiesrealestate.com has even more.

You can find more inspiring luxury lifestyle content online at Luxury Defined: visit for home tours, property galleries, and the best in art, design, wine, travel, and more.

❯ luxurydefined.com

CONTENTS

GREG FUNNELL

44

62

LAURA BARISONZI; BKKARCHITECTS

24

66

CONTRIBUTORS

Greg Funnell
London, UK
Puts a bespoke spectacles maker in the frame (p20)
Funnell studied history and war studies in college before picking up his camera. Today he shoots for the likes of *Vanity Fair* and *The Sunday Times Magazine*. When not at work he can be found upcyling objects in his shed.
Who's your favorite artist?
"I've just discovered the work of Sergio Larrain. I feel like when photography becomes poetry it really drifts into the realm of art."
Which is your favorite gallery and why do you like it?
"I've always enjoyed visiting Polka Gallery in Paris and Foam in Amsterdam. Both show classic contemporary photography. I also love any gallery that has a good bookshop."

David Waters
New York, USA
Looks at the link between fashion and art (p80)
Waters has written about style for the likes of *The Daily Telegraph* and *The Guardian* in his native UK and the *Observer* in New York, the city he now calls home.
Who is your favorite designer?
"Rei Kawakubo at Comme des Garçons. She is a true visionary. You never know what she will come up with next. Her clothes, even those from 25 years ago, always look totally modern."
What's the most fashion-conscious thing you've ever done?
"I once gave a boyfriend a pair of metallic gold shorts I'd found at a market stall. I sewed a Vivienne Westwood label onto them—I couldn't afford the real thing."

John L Walters
London, UK
Examines the world's finest wine labels (p44)
The editor and co-owner of *Eye*, the international review of graphic design, has also written for *The Architectural Review*, *The Guardian*, *The Independent* and *The Wire*. A former musician and record producer, Walters has also organised many design events including *Eye*'s regular Type Tuesday at London's St Bride Library.
What's your favorite piece of design, and what do you like about it?
"My Japanese-made Midori ballpoint pen. It's the perfect writing tool for the extensive notes I take wherever I go."
How would you describe your personal style?
"European. Eclectic."

Laura Barisonzi
New York, USA
Shoots one of fashion's favorite illustrators (p24)
Barisonzi's diverse portfolio includes work for *Rolling Stone*, *The Guardian*, and *Cartier*. When not behind the lens she can be found "biking, running, climbing, swimming, and getting lost abroad."
Who's your favorite photographer?
"Sebastião Salgado. He's a powerful yet sensitive photojournalist and creates truly iconic images. He always has a powerful message behind his work."
What's the secret to a great photo?
"Care about what you shoot. Make the viewer care."
If you could shoot one person, alive or dead, who would it be?
"The Virgin Mary."

CONTACTS

FOR CHRISTIE'S INTERNATIONAL REAL ESTATE Kaysha Velarde-Wilson. magazine@christiesrealestate.com
EDITORIAL Kitty Finstad, Steven Short, Eva Peaty, Emilee Tombs, Laura Hill, Sarah Bravo **ART** Michael Branthwaite
PICTURES Lisa Jacobs **PRODUCTION** David Sharman, James Taggart **PROPERTY LISTINGS** Emma Johnston, Helen Chadney,
Kat Halstead, Natasha Scharf **PUBLISHING** August, a trading division of Publicis Limited. Liz Silvester,
Lee Behan. 82 Baker Street, London W1U 6AE, +44 (0)20 7830 3743, info@augustmedia.com
ADVERTISING magazine@christiesrealestate.com
SUBSCRIPTIONS Christie's International Real Estate, +1 212 468 7182, subscriptions@christiesrealestate.com

Huang Shao-Ning. Startup investor and co-founder of AngelCentral.

What if I live to 100?

Should I make life simpler?
Do I have the right plan?

Life in later years changes. You may want to remain hands on. Take a step back. Or pursue other passions. As time goes by, you might need to reconsider your financial plan. Through careful investment strategies, we can work together to navigate whatever the future holds. Here's to a long, healthy, and fulfilling life.

For some of life's questions, you're not alone. Together we can find an answer.

ANDY WARHOL (1928-1987)
Blackglama (Judy Garland), from *Ads*
unique screenprint in colors, 1985
signed in pencil, numbered 'TP 16/30'
$70,000-100,000

PRINTS & MULTIPLES
New York, 22 & 23 October

VIEWING
18-21 October
20 Rockefeller Plaza
New York, NY 10020

CONTACT
Lindsay Griffith
lgriffith@christies.com
+1 212 336 2290

CHRISTIE'S

GALLERY

Your luxury living edit—interiors, design, art, architecture, and style

Lighting

ROSE REVIVAL

The original Artichoke lights were designed by **Poul Henningsen** for the Langelinie Pavilion restaurant in Copenhagen in 1958. They are still hanging there today. To mark 125 years since Henningsen's birth, **Louis Poulsen** has released a new version of the PH Artichoke, in copper and rose—the dual finish of those original lamps. Henningsen's iconic design consists of a structure of 12 steel arches on which 72 leaves are placed in six overlapping rows. The design means you can admire the complexity of the shade without being able to see the source.

louispoulsen.com

Homewares
View finders

They say good things come in threes. A fine example are these convex mirrors from homewares company **Ochre**. In gesso and burnished bole frames, the mirrors offer a fish-eye view of your home, and the set of three includes a small, medium, and large mirror. They can also be bought separately in sizes ranging from 12 inches (30 cm) in diameter to 41 inches (105 cm), leaving you free to group as you wish. The modular Eternal Dreamer sofa and Arctic Pear chandelier, both pictured, are also by Ochre.
ochre.net

Furniture
OPEN ALL HOURS

The Bookscape Coffee Table by Washington, DC's **Trey Jones Studio** is just what your coffee-table books have been waiting for. Alongside its flat surface areas, with inlaid marble coasters, the table has a sloping marble insert upon which to place your book, open at the desired page. The table's dimensions can be customized, as can the choice of wood, stain, and marble inserts.
treyjonesstudio.com

REST EASY

What do you get when two design worlds collide? The Lounge Chair JH97 is the fruit of an alliance between **Fritz Hansen** of Denmark and Spain's **Jaime Hayon**. "The idea was to create a 'typical' Danish lounge chair, expressive and modern," says Hayon. "Comfort was a key factor, as was the combination of the best of Danish design tradition and modern technology." The chair has a low-slung silhouette, with exaggerated armrests and generously sized cushions lending a contemporary feel. *fritzhansen.com*

Fashion

Tailored to you

"Women have always been an afterthought in tailoring," says **Daisy Knatchbull** of **The Deck**, "but I wanted to bring them the same level of service and quality their male counterparts have been experiencing for years." Quietly launched this year, The Deck is a made-to-measure tailoring brand that focuses exclusively on women. Drawing on the craft of bespoke tailoring, it offers four distinct silhouettes (The Heart, The Spade, The Club, and, you guessed it, The Diamond) that can be customized to their wearer's shape, size, and lifestyle. "The empowering nature of a suit is something every woman should experience in her lifetime," believes Knatchbull. "Tailored suits will always be a wardrobe investment."
thedecklondon.com

Embroidery

THREAD COUNTS

When **Jacky Puzey** couldn't find anyone to
embroider her creations to the high standard
she wanted, she decided to invest in digital
technology and do it herself. The London-based
designer-maker now combines the tech with
traditional embroidery skills to create one-off
and limited-edition pieces of furniture that, in
her own words, "explore a baroque pleasure in
imagery and style." Puzey's designs often feature
the animal kingdom, and she uses feathers, lace,
tweed, and organza in her work. Recent pieces
include an ottoman, complete with preening
peacocks and cheeky squirrels; footstools awash
with koi carp; and this cocktail chair, from
which parakeets appear to take flight (available
exclusively from London Connoisseur).
jackypuzey.com

Furniture

Set to dazzle

As the name suggests, the Ring table mimics jewelry
fittings as they await their precious stones. Available in
copper, brass, steel, and nickel, each table is finished
with a clear or lightly colored tempered-glass top that
is "set" onto the base structure, just as a jewel is set in
a ring. **Saba**, the Italian company that produces the
tables, was established in 1987 and works with top
designers on its collections. For Ring, it teamed up
with Milan-based **Serena Confalonieri**.
sabaitalia.it

Ceramics
TIGHT SQUEEZE

Part sculptural object, part vase or bowl, the Veer ceramic vessels are the fruit of a collaboration between **Straight Design Studio** of Stockholm and Swedish designer **Samir Dzabirov**. "We wanted to play with shapes and function," says the studio's Viktor Erlandsson. "Create something in movement without any visible beginning or end. Change direction to change function." The wider end of the speckled object works as a bowl, flip it and you get a vase.
straightdesign.se

Woodwork
Totem gesture

"I love the figure-like forms of [Romanian sculptor] Brâncuși and was heavily influenced by his scale and experimental use of negative space," says **Peg Woodworking**'s **Kate Casey** of her Totem collection. Part sculpture, part one-off piece of furniture, each Totem is a unique coopered stack that can be used to display favorite objects, or simply left bare as an artful ornament. There is a Totem coffee table, too—the stack, in this case, laid on its side—in bleached and ebonized ash with a silver wave marble top. "With the pieces, scale and orientation is infinitely rearrangeable, allowing them to interact with each other and their surroundings," says the Brooklyn-based woodworker and designer.
pegwoodworking.com

Tiles

SHAPE SHIFTING

Launched in the centennial year of the Bauhaus movement—known for its love
of geometric shapes—**Alison Rose**'s Euclid tiles are aptly named after the father
of geometry. Crafted from classic European marbles, the tiles can be customized
in both colorway and composition. Created for **Artistic Tile**, "the collection was
inspired by studying tapestries under a microscope, interpreting the sequence of
fibers into a geometric format," says Rose, who describes the tiles as "set units
designed to work together in an infinite number of ways to tell your story."
artistictile.com

Interiors

An air of suspense

Mathieu Lehanneur says he has often dreamed of a world without gravity, "like a floating state where the notions of heavy and light have no more meanings." The Parisian designer has taken this idea as inspiration for his new Inverted Gravity collection—tables, seating, and storage comprised of slabs of marble and onyx resting on bubbles of blown glass, as if suspended in air. The collection combines state-of-the-art technology with expert craftsmanship to bring strength and resistance to seemingly fragile forms. *mathieulehanneur.com*

New horizons

Designed by **Giuseppe Bavuso** for Italian company **Alivar**, the Horizon has tilted armrests and backrests for a more comfortable seating position. Plumply upholstered, the steel-and-wood-framed sofa features dainty legs in painted cast aluminum, and three cushions for total loungeability. *alivar.com*

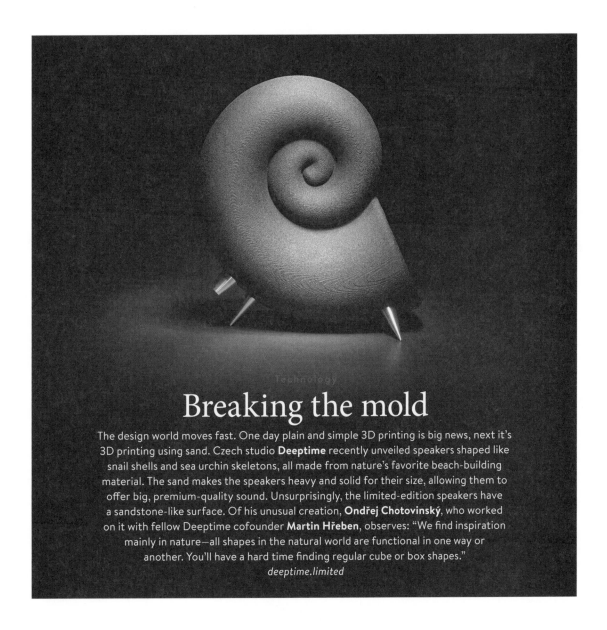

Technology

Breaking the mold

The design world moves fast. One day plain and simple 3D printing is big news, next it's 3D printing using sand. Czech studio **Deeptime** recently unveiled speakers shaped like snail shells and sea urchin skeletons, all made from nature's favorite beach-building material. The sand makes the speakers heavy and solid for their size, allowing them to offer big, premium-quality sound. Unsurprisingly, the limited-edition speakers have a sandstone-like surface. Of his unusual creation, **Ondřej Chotovinský**, who worked on it with fellow Deeptime cofounder **Martin Hřeben**, observes: "We find inspiration mainly in nature—all shapes in the natural world are functional in one way or another. You'll have a hard time finding regular cube or box shapes."
deeptime.limited

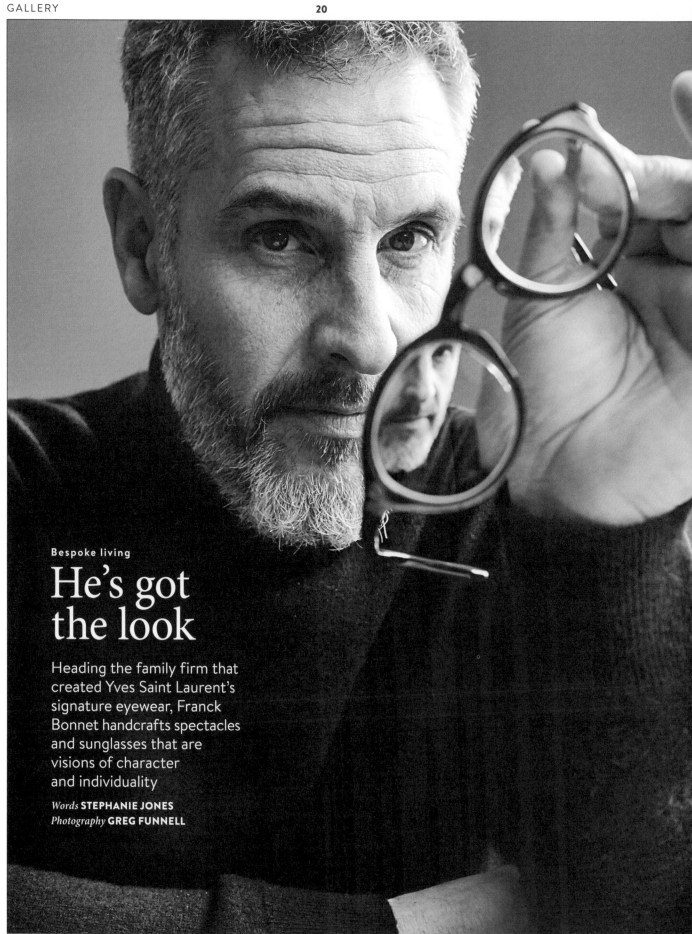

Bespoke living

He's got
the look

Heading the family firm that
created Yves Saint Laurent's
signature eyewear, Franck
Bonnet handcrafts spectacles
and sunglasses that are
visions of character
and individuality

Words **STEPHANIE JONES**
Photography **GREG FUNNELL**

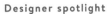

Out there: Sasha Bikoff (*top right*), describes her style as "Marie Antoinette at Studio 54." Her designs include the Versace x Sasha Bikoff collection, launched at this year's Milan Design Week (*top*), a Hudson Valley residence (*above*), and the Stairway to Heaven installation at the Kips Bay Decorator Show House 2018 (*right*).

Designer spotlight

Sasha Bikoff

A career detour led the musician into a different world—creating stunning interiors inspired by French Rococo and space-age Modernism

Looking at any of her eclectic interior designs, you would never guess that Sasha Bikoff was self-taught. The New Yorker was headed for a career as a singer—she secured a record deal at 18—before her grandfather encouraged her to go to college instead. Music was put aside in favor of fine art and painting, but it was overhauling the interior of her mother's home in the iconic Dakota building that cemented her destiny as a designer.

"My mom had gone through two designers who couldn't understand what she wanted, so I told her I was going to do her apartment," says Bikoff. "The project went viral and the rest is history."

Prior to this, Bikoff had worked at the Gagosian gallery in New York, and also spent time in Paris, living in the apartment of acclaimed designer Lisa Fine. "I walked into the apartment and the fabric walls matched the fabric headboard that matched the lampshades and the carpets. I felt like I had just walked into a jewel box."

Back in New York, Bikoff learned the interiors business from the ground up. "I never worked with an interior designer at a firm. I walked around the city acquainting myself with all of the fabric and furniture showrooms. Now I have it down to a science—but I had to teach myself." *sashabikoff.com*

In the studio with...

Blair Breitenstein

The illustrator's instantly recognizable portraits and vignettes are inspired by
a lifelong love of fashion magazines and contemporary couture

Words **STEVEN SHORT**   *Photography* **LAURA BARISONZI**

Ask Blair Breitenstein who she would most like to immortalize in one of her quirky, fun illustrations and her answer is unequivocal. "Anna Wintour. I love drawing someone with a signature look; you can use your artistic license but the subject is still recognizable. I love Anna."

Fashion has always loomed large in the Seattle-born, NYC-based illustrator's life. Her grandmother worked for a clothing company and Breitenstein was fascinated by the lookbooks, sketches, and fabric swatches she kept on her desk. "And I loved looking through fashion magazines. My grandma had subscriptions to *Town & Country* and *W*; I always took her old issues home with me."

Drawing from an early age, Breitenstein majored in communications and advertising at college, with a fine art minor. "I always thought I would work in advertising. But I started posting my drawings on Tumblr after college and people were interested in buying them." Surprised by this commerciality, she began drawing fashion for a living. An early commission, for Oscar de la Renta, meant going backstage at a runway show where, "I completely fell in love with the artistic atmosphere."

Today Breitenstein works from her home. "I usually set up a spot on the floor or couch. I like being able to draw at any time, and I draw very quickly when I feel inspired," creating instantly recognizable portraits and vignettes in markers, pastels, and watercolors. As well as working commercially, she sells original and limited-edition prints on her website, describing her prodigious output as "an expressionist take on contemporary high fashion."

When not creating, the artist will be on Instagram, screenshotting images that inspire her or feeding her 116,000 followers. "Instagram gave me a platform to share my artwork with important people in the fashion industry," she says. "I tag designers and editors who I admire, with hopes that they will see what I do."

Breitenstein has worked for Alexander McQueen and Louis Vuitton, but is always looking for new collaborations. "I'd love to create a textile," she says, "ideally for Prada, or Miu Miu—favorite brand ever!" *blairabreitenstein.com*

Opposite: Blair Breitenstein's "expressionist" work is influenced by high-fashion photography. *Below, from left:* Limited-edition print *Valentino 19*; watercolors, markers, and pastels suit her quick, quirky style; the late Karl Lagerfeld with his cat, Choupette.

Has architecture always interested you? From an early age I had a passion for making things: jewelry, books, clothes, drawings. It is this interest in creation that underlies my passion for architecture, whereas James knew from a very young age that he wanted to design.

Why did you and your husband decide to team up professionally? We knew we shared an aligned vision as well as a passion for design—we had already been married 13 years and worked on the same projects while at different offices. There was a long-term goal of uniting professionally and this came into focus on 9/11. We lived and worked near the Twin Towers and were parking our car under one of them when the first plane hit—this crystallized the brevity of our lives. We formalized our firm 12 months later and established Slade Architecture in 2002.

You coauthored some design guidelines for affordable housing in NYC; why do you think architects have a responsibility in this area? Housing is one of the fundamental human needs that we are qualified to address professionally, as architects. We feel it is an ethical responsibility to apply that expertise to the pressing social challenges of our time. The vast majority of NYC community boards list adequate affordable housing as their top priority. We are long-term New Yorkers and feel a deep civic responsibility to our city.

What makes a home work in terms of architecture and design? A home that works will foster the lifestyle that the family wants to have. A home also has an obligation to its physical and social context, whether a farm, suburb, or city block. So, flexible designs that can grow with the family; focused views to the landscape; and living spaces designed to easily accommodate gatherings and entertaining.

Clockwise from top left: Shanghai's flagship Barbie store; Link Farm House in Stanford, New York; the streetscape-inspired lobby at an apartment block in NYC's Lower East Side; custom furniture at a vacation home in South Beach, Miami, built using surfboard technology; the Virgin Atlantic Clubhouse at JFK Airport references the glamour of 1960s air travel; Greene Street Loft in NYC.

Architect Q&A

Slade Architecture

New York-based architect Hayes Slade, who went into business with her husband James after a close call on 9/11 hastened their plans, seeks to improve relationships and ultimately society through a passion for design

IWAN BANN; TOM SIBLEY; JORDI MIRALLES; KEN HAYDEN; ANTON STARK

What is the Slade style of working? Neat, with impact and heart. Our passion for design is rooted in a desire to improve relationships, and ultimately society. Architecture is always in the service of relationships, with neighbors, passersby, the community in general.

How do you begin working on a project? We begin with dialogue and research. We start with a thorough investigation of our client, their desires and goals, as well as the context in which the project will exist.

What unites your works? No matter the variety of unique contextual conditions, which tend to lead to distinct designs, all our projects look at how occupants perceive and experience the space. We often create conditions of perceptual ambiguity to encourage engagement between the occupant and the building.

Tell us about your clients… Our mix of projects includes residential, retail, hospitality, and institutional. Several are with clients we have worked with over many years—it is wonderful to deepen the relationship and continue our investigation of design together.

If you could live anywhere, where would you choose? We can imagine enjoying so many places and ways to live. That being said, cities offer such rich diversity that we tend to be drawn to urban conditions for long-term residence. A row house in the West Village of NYC or in London would be high on our list.

What does home mean to you? A place we return to time and again with loved ones. *sladearch.com*

The world of Christie's

News and expert insight from the auction house

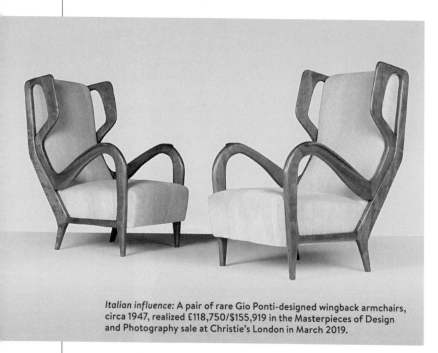

Italian influence: A pair of rare Gio Ponti-designed wingback armchairs, circa 1947, realized £118,750/$155,919 in the Masterpieces of Design and Photography sale at Christie's London in March 2019.

Christie's Education

Italian Modern Art and Design course

Italy has been at the forefront of the design world for more than 100 years, with countless works making their way into the design pantheon. On October 4, Christie's London will hold the Thinking Italian sale, showcasing Italian masterpieces of design. To coincide with the sale, Christie's Education will host **An Introduction to Italian Modern Art and Design**, a two-day course revealing the artists and designers behind iconic Italian objects. The course will also look at how Italy became a leading influence on the post-war scene. Highlights will include key designers of the 20th century, including Gio Ponti, Carlo Mollino, and Ettore Sottsass, along with an interactive session discussing and handling pieces included in the Christie's Italian sale.
christies.edu

The wine expert

BUYING BEFORE BOTTLING

Chris Munro, Head of Wine Department, Americas, Christie's New York

Buying Bordeaux *en primeur* means buying a wine before it is bottled, a practice that began after World War II when the châteaux were in crisis. Short of money, they sold their wines in-barrel to leading *négociants* of the time. Following several disappointing vintages and the mid-1970s oil crisis, they expanded sales to merchants in the UK and northern Europe. By acquiring large stocks, vendors were able to offer wines to their clients at reasonable prices, for delivery two years later. The great change came with the 1982 vintage—seen as the best since 1961. It also saw Americans enter the *en primeur* market, and the emergence of wine critic Robert Parker, whose "Parker points" often decided release prices. In superb vintages, demand was immense. Prices were attractive enough for buyers to make major gains on wines bought as futures, and while the last great investment vintage was 2008, *en primeur* remains a great way to secure wine. Attend the tastings, usually held in March following the vintage, and read all the reports you can. There are often great wines known as "sleepers" to be found in unheralded vintages. But only buy from reputable vendors: you are buying for the future, so make sure the merchant will still be around then.

Good investment: Twelve bottles of Château Angélus 2010 sold for $4,375 in the Finest & Rarest Wines and Spirits sale at Christie's New York in June 2019.

Clockwise from left: A black crocodile Passe-Guide; a limited-edition Osier Picnic Garden Party; a custom Bleu Tempête and Prune horseshoe-stamped Sellier Kelly; a limited-edition Vert Émeraude and Vert Titien patchwork Birkin 30; a Kelly Pochette in Rose Azalée.

A Christie's expert on…

Hermès bags

Caitlin Donovan, Vice President, Head of Sale, Handbags & Accessories, Christie's New York

Hoping to procure your first vintage collectible treasure, or add the most sought-after unicorn on the secondary handbags market to your extensive collection? New York-based expert Caitlin Donovan introduces her favorite Hermès bags from Christie's 2019 Handbags & Accessories spring auction season, many of which exceeded their estimates, proving the ongoing desirability of the brand.

COLLECTION STARTERS
Among the most collectible of Hermès' limited-edition bags are the **Osier** pieces, often fetching record prices in the saleroom. Perfect for a summer's day and evoking the bohemian spirit of Jane Birkin, the **Osier Picnic Garden Party** (pictured top left) is a very special collector's item, at an entry-level price. In May, the bag realized HK$106,250/US$13,594 against a HK$20,000–$30,000 estimate.

Potentially more accessible still is the multicolor canvas **Après Le Surf** tote (not pictured). Perfect for outdoor pursuits, it nods to the brand's sporting heritage. Both playful and functional, and large enough to carry all beach essentials, it is made of sturdy canvas to withstand the surf and sand. More importantly, one such tote is available in the upcoming November Online sale, with a low estimate of just $500.

MIDWEIGHT MARVELS
Petite handbags have, in recent years, been crowned the most coveted of collectible handbags on the secondary market. The **Kelly Pochette** has been a favorite of collectors of Hermès since the model's creation, and here (below) it's perfectly executed in a bright and cheerful Rose Azalée hue and structured Epsom leather. A standout piece from the May/June Online sale, it sold for $27,500 against an estimate of $4,000-$6,000.

Originally introduced in 1975, the **Passe-Guide** was re-released in 2012. Named for its clasp, inspired by the ring on the front of a Roman chariot, the Passe-Guide was the most expensive bag to be released at its inception. The model pictured above left, in a classic black-and-gold combination, sold in June for £9,375/$11,878 against a £5,000–£7,000 estimate.

THE SHOWSTOPPERS
The saleroom is often the only place to find one-of-a-kind creations such as the horseshoe-stamped **Sellier Kelly** (top). With a bicolor exterior in Bleu Tempête and Prune, and with brushed palladium hardware, this bag has a unique identity that more than justifies its $17,500 hammer price in the May/June Online sale.

The patchwork **Birkin 30** shown above features five coveted Hermès colors and six different skins, the complementary combination proof of Hermès' exquisite craftsmanship, eye for detail, and high level of quality. The bag's flap closure is crafted from the finest exotic skin used by the brand, shiny Porosus crocodile, while the remainder of the bag combines classic Hermès materials such as Epsom, Clémence, Evercolor, Calf Box, and Chèvre leathers. The piece realized HK$400,000/US$51,178 in May.

**THE COLLECTION OF
LEE BOUVIER RADZIWILL**
New York, 17 October 2019

VIEWING
11-16 October 2019
20 Rockefeller Plaza
New York, NY 10020

CONTACT
Elizabeth Seigel
eseigel@christies.com
+1 212 636 2229

CHRISTIE'S

TRAVEL

Hotel news, the hottest destinations, and how to get there in style

WORDS: EMILEE TOMBS. PHOTOGRAPHY: RON BLUNT

Washington, DC, USA

MAKING HEADLINES AGAIN

The Watergate Hotel made waves thanks to its groundbreaking design when it opened in 1961, and then came *that* scandal in 1972. Today, it's back in the news after an overhaul by architect Ron Arad, whose mid-century-style interiors are complemented by staff uniforms from *Mad Men* costume designer Janie Bryant. The Next Whisky Bar is a must-visit thanks to its curvaceous wall displaying 2,500 illuminated bottles, and its 260-plus whiskies, bourbons, and ryes. Gourmets will love fine-dining restaurant Kingbird, serving a seasonal menu of American classics with French accents. And Room 214—the Scandal Room—features 1970s memorabilia and walls hung with original news clippings from the day the scandal broke.
thewatergatehotel.com

Ballyfin, Ireland

REGENCY REGENERATED

A vast 19th-century Irish manor, **Ballyfin** may have been magicked into a five-star hotel, but it remains a country house at heart. At the top of a winding drive, set within 614 acres (248 ha) of parkland, the house appears, its Neoclassical façade austere yet beautiful. Inside, 35,000 square feet (3,252 sq m) of Greek Revival architecture, Roman mosaics, Moorish marquetry, and Empire decor await.

The decorative diversity is a nod to the Grand Tour tradition of former owners, the Coote family, when travelers returned from Europe with a rich collection of artifacts. In the Gold Drawing Room, the silk damask wall covering was rewoven using an original salvaged scrap. And in the 20 unique bedrooms there are domed canopy beds, marble tubs and fireplaces, and 17th-century tapestries.

Alongside such elegance, a warm atmosphere prevails. Guests are encouraged to fully explore the grounds, and rest weary legs on a plush sofa. And the "butlers"—concierges, coachmen, and activities managers all in one—underline the sense that this is not a hotel at all, but a wonderful, private home. *ballyfin.com*

WORDS: KATHRYN ANDERSON

WORDS: EMILEE TOMBS

Paris, France

Best in class

In Paris, the Distinction Palace classification is reserved for just 11 hotels, considering attributes such as location, legacy, character, staff excellence, restaurants, respect for the environment, and more. Those that achieve this accolade are in a class of their own, and **The Peninsula Paris** is among them.

Its location, on Avenue Kléber, couldn't be better. Sitting at the heart of Paris's Golden Triangle, with the city's most famous monuments a short stroll away, the hotel's 200 rooms and suites are inspired by haute couture and are among the largest in Paris.

With The Peninsula Hotels group an official partner of Art Basel Hong Kong, it's no surprise that celebrating art is central to its ethos. And from September to November, guests at The Peninsula Paris will be able to view pieces from the Hong Kong launch of the group's Art in Resonance program, alongside new installations from local artists. Expect boundary-pushing work by the likes of Iván Navarro, Saya Woolfalk, and Elise Morin, curated by art-world tastemakers Isolde Brielmaier and Bettina Prentice.
peninsula.com/en/paris

GETTY IMAGES

Italy

A TALE OF TWO CITIES

Rome and Florence are within easy reach of each other,
yet offer distinctly different vacation experiences

Words **EMILEE TOMBS AND STEVEN SHORT**

DESIGNER'S HAVEN
JK Place Roma

In a city as beguiling as Rome, the temptation is to spend every second of your time here exploring. Yet even in the most enchanting destinations, there will come a time of day when thoughts turn to home comforts. Enter **JK Place Roma**: a home away from home for design lovers. Located on Via di Monte d'Oro—a quiet street just minutes from the throng of the Spanish Steps—this stylish hotel has 30 rooms and suites, and five-star service that helps you truly relax.

On the ground floor, light streams into the lobby lounge through a skylight, illuminating a collection of art and sculpture from across Europe that includes a French plaster statue thought to date from around 1870; a 1970s wood panel by Nerone and Patuzzi, Group NP2; a wall lamp from the 1940s; and soft furnishings by Michele Bönan, who is also the architect of the building's current iteration.

The library has a distinctly mid-century feel, with dark wood paneling and bookcases that house an array of fashion and design tomes. An onyx fireplace, Murano lamps, and gray velvet seating purchased from an out-of-service Dior airplane complete the look, making this an excellent setting for a business meeting—or after-dinner espresso (martini). Adjoining the library, the jewel-toned JK Café serves Sunday brunch, plus a market-fresh

lunch and dinner menu of international and Italian classics. Turn the corner and take a seat in the lounge-bar, where you can watch your favorite team or a classic movie at your leisure—a drink of choice in hand, naturally.

ARTFUL ELEGANCE
JK Place Firenze

It's hard to overstate the beauty of Florence, where every street seems to have a church more exquisite than the last and each gallery and museum an artwork or historical artifact you've waited years to gaze upon. The home of the Renaissance, the city was made for exploring on foot. Make **JK Place Firenze** your base and you'll be at the very heart of Florence and everything it offers.

With just 20 elegant rooms, the hotel is intimate and pleasingly relaxed: paneled walls and high painted ceilings in public areas, and four-poster beds in the airy rooms where calming neutrals are the order of the day. JK hotels have a reputation for helping guests get the most from their visits, and the Florence offering is no exception; from the welcome drink to suggestions for places to eat and drink, a stay here feels like reconnecting with old friends—friends who know their neighborhood inside out. You're even given a copy of *JK Insider Guide to Florence*, curated by general manager and local legend Claudio Meli, when you arrive.

But you don't have to leave the hotel to enjoy excellent Tuscan food. A lavish breakfast spread is served in a glass-domed courtyard (complete with homemade cakes and breads), while the JK Lounge restaurant and bar serves lunches and dinners made with seasonal, locally sourced produce (vegetables come from a nearby farm). You may, in fact, find it hard to leave the hotel. But do venture out, safe in the knowledge that you can end the day with a nightcap on JK's rooftop terrace. *jkplace.com*

Clockwise from bottom left: Relax in JK Place Roma's central lounge area; the Italian capital's Roman Forum; visit the Duomo of Florence for Gothic art at its finest; the intimate breakfast room at JK Place Firenze; a Master Room, with views over Piazza Santa Maria Novella; JK Place Firenze's 20 rooms include two-story suites.

London, UK

ROOM FOR EVERYONE

The first thing you notice at **The Beaumont** is how delicious it smells. Instantly seductive, the fragrance that hangs in the air at this chic London hotel was made specially for its Art Deco-inspired interiors. What you might not notice is the colossal stack of steel cubes and rectangles perched on the southeast façade. Crafted by sculptor Antony Gormley, this is Room: a one-of-a-kind suite into which guests can retreat to an almost monastic-like space.

Elsewhere, beautifully appointed rooms and suites have unique decorative touches: a mirrored panel here, a lacquered bar cabinet there, all with sumptuous upholstery. The five-bedroom Roosevelt suite also features an eight-seat dining room and private terrace.

Whichever accommodation takes your fancy, everyone is sure to delight in the hotel's excellent American bar, The Magritte, whose 1930s ambience has had a "soft refurb" by Nina Campbell. Among the 20th-century posters and paintings, the bar's star artwork is René Magritte's *Le Maître d'École* (1955). *thebeaumont.com*

HISTORY OF
JEWELLERY DESIGN
1880 – NOW

A SIX-WEEK ONLINE COURSE

Explore the glamour and exquisite craftsmanship of
Haute Joaillerie from the Belle Époque to the present day
through six lavishly-produced sessions.

Learn more at christies.edu/online

CHRISTIE'S
EDUCATION

Patek Philippe. A Very Fine and Rare 18k White Gold
Wristwatch
Ref. 3711/1, Manufactured in 2006
$70,000-100,000

IMPORTANT WATCHES

New York, 11 December 2019

VIEWING
December 2019
20 Rockefeller Plaza
New York, NY 10020

CONTACT
Rebecca Ross
rross@christies.com
+ 1 212 636 2323

CHRISTIE'S

GOURMET

Our edit of what's new and newsworthy in the world of fine food, drink, and entertaining

Glassware
SEASON'S BEST

Felicia Ferrone says her favorite month of the year is May, when spring eases into summer. The Chicago-born designer likes the month so much she has created a range of stemmed glasses named in its honor. The elegant May Collection of glassware, with fluted, pillar-shaped bases that nod to Art Deco design, is handcrafted in the Czech Republic by master glassblowers using borosilicate glass. Surprisingly for such delicate barware, the glasses are dishwasher (and microwave) safe.
fferronedesign.com

In the kitchen with…

Simon Rogan

Acclaimed London restaurant Roganic, a pop-up venture by Michelin-starred chef **Simon Rogan**, originally opened in 2011, but ended up staying put for two years. In 2018, Roganic returned to the British capital, joining Aulis, Rogan's eight-seat chef's table-cum-development restaurant, which opened in October 2017. The chef patron has now replicated the Roganic–Aulis model in Hong Kong, in the heart of Causeway Bay. "I opened in Hong Kong as it is one of my favorite cities. It has such an exciting and buzzing food scene," says Rogan. "I went over there for a pop-up and had the chance to make it permanent. The restaurant industry in Hong Kong is always evolving, so I thought it would be perfect for my first international venture." Diners at Roganic Hong Kong (pictured) choose between the eight- or 10-course taster menus—or three-course lunch—which showcase Rogan's love of farm-to-table dishes. Aulis Hong Kong, meanwhile, invites 12 guests at a time to "surrender their senses to the creativity of the chefs" as they sample innovative cooking from an ever-evolving 10-course menu. *simonrogan.co.uk*

HAARALA HAMILTON

SUNNY SIDE UP

What you eat for breakfast used to be dictated by where you grew up, but in the global kitchen you can start your day any which way you choose. *Breakfast: The Cookbook*, by Emily Elyse Miller, is the first book to showcase breakfast recipes from around the world—sweet, savory, regional, or classic—complete with cultural context. From Swedish cardamom buns (left), to Mexican *chilaquiles* (top left) and Tunisian chickpea and torn-bread stew (top right), the recipes prove that breakfast really is the most important meal of the day. *phaidon.com*

Family spirit: Joint managing directors Beanie Geraedts-Espey (*far left*) and Rebecca Jago; The Last Drop Distillers' many rare finds include two casks of a 1969 Glenrothes single-malt Scotch.

Spirits

TREASURE HUNTERS

James Espey, Tom Jago, and Peter Fleck spent their working lives in the spirits business. When the time came to retire they agreed they simply didn't want to, deciding instead to become rare spirit hunters. The venture they founded, **The Last Drop Distillers**—now overseen by two of their daughters, Rebecca Jago and Beanie Geraedts-Espey—seeks out the world's finest, rarest, and most exclusive spirits, bottling them for a growing number of connoisseurs. Among the intoxicating gems the company has so far unearthed are a 1950 aged cognac, found in a tiny distillery in the woods near Cognac, and a 1961 Dumbarton single-grain Scotch whisky. The nature of these discoveries mean editions are extremely limited (just 32 bottles of that 1961 Dumbarton), so the company has also produced a house pour: Tom's Blend No. 1, an 18-year-old blended Scotch with a wisp of smoke from Islay. "It's a harmonious blend," says Rebecca Jago, "created as a tribute to my father, who, until his death last year, would pour himself a dram of fine Scotch blend every evening at 6pm and reflect on the day." Jago, Geraedts-Espey, and their team are also working on a groundbreaking initiative aging bourbon barrels in a carefully controlled environment to try to mimic the temperatures of Scotland. Some will be left untouched, but closely monitored, for up to 50 years.
lastdropdistillers.com

Accessories

DRESSED TO PERFECTION

Whether it's cupcakes or chateaubriand that you're preparing, a good apron is essential. **Witloft** aprons are made by hand in Holland using the finest leather, with many designs finished with a unique coating that protects the apron from stains, dirt, and the worst scratches. They are wipe-clean and work well in heated environments—like standing in front of the barbecue. Customers have the option of personalizing their apron, too; choose your favorite skin color, then add straps and details such as your name, initials, or a date. Witloft also produces handy leather pockets that can be attached to its aprons, as well as leather knife rolls. *witloft.com*

Entertaining

The mark of excellence

With hand-blown crystal champagne flutes inspired by V12 engines, caviar and blini caissons, and champagne coolers in black anodized aluminum and carbon fiber, the **Rolls-Royce** Champagne Chest is the ideal gift for those who like a touch of showmanship with their alfresco wining and dining. At the touch of a button, the chest opens to reveal a champagne set for four guests, its lid metamorphosizing into a beautiful serving tray made of Tudor oak with a laser-cut stainless-steel inlay. Four cotton napkins embroidered with the Rolls-Royce "RR" monogram—a symbol of precision design—are also included, as are mother-of-pearl spoons for the caviar. *rolls-roycemotorcars.com*

The art of temptation:
Paying homage to
regional folklore,
wolves take center
stage in Domaine La
Louvière's black and
white illustrations,
which also nod toward
eroticism with names
such as La Séductrice,
part of the vineyard's
"temptations" range,
and Le Libertin, in its
"pleasures" collection.

VINTAGE DESIGN

*Clever vintners know that how a bottle
looks in the 21st century is almost as
important as what's inside. We raise
a glass to the modern wine label*

Words **JOHN L WALTERS**

To see a gallery of design in all its delicious glory,
look no further than your local wine store.
Alongside wine labels that have changed little in
centuries, you will see Surrealism, photomontage,
Constructivism, bold portraiture, capricious illustration,
and every kind of typography from tasteful serifs to
flamboyant Tuscan fonts. Wine shelves are as graphically
vibrant as record stores and bookshops used to be.

Some labels, such as the groundbreaking "electro" labels
designed by Xavier Bas for Tomàs Cusiné, are mesmerizing
abstract images that draw you in, whispering "drink me" in
a seductive Catalan accent. Others, such as Harry Pearce's
text-only labels for centuries-old wine business Berry
Brothers & Rudd (BBR), provide the cool reassurance of
French wines in an English cellar. Ryan DiDonato's literal
illustrations for Il Palagio, the vineyard co-owned by
musician Sting, make a link between wine and nostalgia,
while Fernando Gutiérrez's forthright letterforms for
Telmo Rodríguez communicate uncompromising quality.

INFORM AND INSPIRE

What fills the label space has to work hard—telling you
what the wine is, and persuading you to buy it, too. Paula
Macfarlane, who for several years designed supermarket
wine labels for creative agency Lewis Moberly, says: "The
client is always looking to stand out on the shelf, rather
than wanting a description of the wine or heritage."

Wine expert Paul Keers, former editor of *GQ*, and
cofounder of the Sediment blog, notes how wine has
become an increasingly mass-market commodity: "That
has made labels louder and more garish, relying on humor,

Left and above: Label styles may vary across Il Palagio's bottles, but all wines are named after songs made famous by vineyard co-owner Sting.

Above right: Known for specializing in signage, exhibition, and packaging design, Fernando Gutiérrez has been creating labels for Telmo Rodríguez for amost 20 years.

loud graphics, and bright colors." Conversely, upmarket labels rarely think in terms of competing visually. "They know they will be sought out, whereas the mass-market wines are competing for attention on a shelf," he observes.

"My favorite wine labels are the early Mouton Rothschilds, the artists' versions," says Macfarlane. "The use of red to pick out various words or initials within the block of black script or sans-serif type… they are charming." Others cite the Picasso or Chagall labels for Mouton Rothschild as the gold standard.

Pearce, who works for Pentagram, the world's largest independent design consultancy, emphasizes the importance of honoring tradition and longevity in his designs for BBR. "[British supermarket] Waitrose changes design strategy every 18 months; BBR has

a 25-year business plan," he says. BBR's creative director Geordie Willis continues: "We were keen to bring a sense of place to each label in the same way that great wines express their *terroir.* We did this by visiting geographically and historically relevant fonts for each wine." Pearce spent weeks in BBR's historic cellars on London's St James's Street, plus BBR sent him on a wine-appreciation course.

Gutiérrez has been designing for Basque Country's Telmo Rodríguez for almost two decades. The elegant labels are not literal, but take their cue from conversations about the region, the land, and the sustainable methods of harvesting. Gutiérrez's earthy colors are reminiscent of the ground from which the vines spring, while his letter Ms—letterpress-printed by Alan Kitching—hint at the artisan winemaking process. "A vineyard is a simple business that works in a very natural way," observes Gutiérrez. Telmo Rodríguez, he says, "is into the whole culture of wine. We look at how we can communicate the wine, just to do justice to it."

Such long-term relationships are not unusual. Bas, the doyen of Catalan wine label design since breaking »

Capturing an essence: For Motif Wines (left and above), Austrian agency En Garde set out to create a "sixth sense," transforming the taste and smell of each wine into an eyecatching pattern; in labels for Matsu (below) and biodynamic producer Gut Oggau (right), portraiture is used to convey the personality and character of the wine.

through with Tomàs Cusiné, says he has never lost a client. Design Bridge's Graham Shearsby has worked with Marqués de Riscal since the brand began 33 years ago, and values the intimacy of their relationship. "Our first meeting [in 1986] was around the family kitchen table eating lamb chops and home-grown broad beans… and a wine from 1924," he recalls. Design Bridge's label work also includes a range for Fortnum & Mason and for Château d'Esclans, another relationship that goes back more than 20 years.

There is also the business of selling wine to people who know little about wine, as opposed to those who know everything. The Motif Wines range, designed by Austria's En Garde agency, uses a combination of tasting notes and eye-catching geometrics to entice and educate young drinkers. The wines' names use dialect terms, such as *zslempat* and *gschniglt* (the former means chaotic or immoral; the latter clean and elegant) from the Southern Styrian region of Austria in which the wine is made.

INDIVIDUAL CHARACTER
For its southern French wines, Domaine La Louvière engaged Austrian art director Cordula Alessandri and illustrator Florine Glück to make slyly erotic labels which hint that its wines—with names such as Le Libertin and La Séductrice—might be wolves in dandies' clothing.

Another trend is the use of faces. Design studio Moruba's labels for Spanish organic winery Matsu feature artisans whose soulful eyes follow you around the cellar. "The faces reflect something of the earthy, authentic quality of the wine," says Keers. Further examples of "face labels" can be seen in the Romanian Minima Moralia wines, and in the Gut Oggau portraits designed by Jung von Matt: bearded hipster Joschuari for a red and matriarch Mechthild for white, both members of an imaginary family.

Personality and humor undoubtedly work: Pentagram's labels for BBR's wholesale wines make spirited use of

Left: **Designs by Xavier Bas for Bodega Biniagual and Tomàs Cusiné.**

Above and below: **Pared-back typography and visual puns add a modern twist to tradition in labels for centuries-old business Berry Brothers & Rudd.**

EN GARDE

words, with visual puns such as "One more river to cross," dizzying typographic cocktails ("Pietas"), and a typewritten poem for "Eternal Return Rosado."

Some wine labels exemplify Bas's thoughts about the sector. "Many clients are now more focused on tradition and value than on identity and authenticity," he says, "which is not so strange if you think about politics in Europe!" He enthusiastically shows off his latest, undeniably "authentic," label for a new client, who he says is extremely passionate about her land. The small vineyard (Pla de Tudela) is in Salvador Dalí country, near Costa Brava in Catalonia. Bas commissioned UK-based illustrator David Hewitt to fly over and spend three days drawing the landscape. The resulting pencil drawings, spare and appealing, form the basis of an identity design and labels for a new winemaker about to make her mark on the world. "These smaller companies often have very few people working for them, no marketing or advertising," says Bas, "so we have to think about everything!" ●

John L Walters is founder and editor of international graphic design journal Eye. *He is also an author and composer*

A NEW
WORLD

This sophisticated, contemporary wine
estate in Napa Valley pairs striking design
with fruitful *terroir* to create a Wine
Country offering without compare

Words **ANDREA HUNT**
Photography **DANE TASHIMA**

Step outside: Impeccably designed to make the most of Napa Valley's temperate climate and scenic landscape, the stylish main home is wrapped in terraces that include 2,775 square feet (257 sq m) of covered living space.

Natural selection: Despite its scale, the estate sits quietly within its setting thanks to the architect's use of natural materials and subdued hues, inside and out. Carefully chosen custom finishes and furnishings elevate the understated aesthetic.

When it comes to connoisseurs of fine wine, there are staunch, Old World traditionalists and those who champion the allure and innovation of the new. Nestled in the heart of Napa Valley, northern California, deep in Wine Country, Whitehall Estate is a glorious celebration of all things new. In a region where much of the architecture echoes old-world style, from the grand châteaux of Bordeaux to the sprawling villas of Tuscany, this elegant seven-bedroom estate on an ultra-secluded plot of 20 acres (8 ha) is no pale imitation. That makes it a rare find indeed.

A stunning example of contemporary design by Bay Area architect Lewis Butler, built over five years, it offers sleek lines, exquisite craftsmanship, utter privacy, and seamless indoor–outdoor living. Sliding glass walls imbue the interiors with golden California sunshine and captivating, all-encompassing vistas over the estate's 14 acres (5.6 ha) of vineyards and beyond to vine-clad slopes, knolls, and the Mayacamas Mountains. The stone exteriors are pared back and in tune with the local landscape. And the interiors are open-plan and welcoming, with rich neutral tones reflecting the natural surroundings.

Step outside and the sun-drenched terraces, infinity-edge pool, pavilion, and grounds invite you to savor the temperate

climate and linger over enchanting views as the sun's trajectory casts shifting shadows through endless rows of vines. "Everyone in California talks about indoor–outdoor living but I've never seen a home that encapsulates the ethos more graciously than this one," says Zackary Wright, Executive Director for Asia Pacific and Western North America at Christie's International Real Estate. "Whereas in other Napa Valley estates you may get certain vantage points for appreciating beautiful views, the experience of this property is one of truly living with the vines. There is no place on the estate where you aren't immersed in them."

BALANCED BLEND

Like a distinctive glass of Rutherford Bench Cabernet Sauvignon, the estate unfolds with confident, compelling character. The four-bedroom main residence opens with the embodiment of the architect's vision of a "modern vineyard masterpiece": a suspended wine cellar, encased in glass, that provides a view through to the estate's vines. It's the spirit and beauty of Napa Valley, from grapes to glass. As befits a home here, where life is all about gourmet food and wine, the residence centers on the expertly crafted kitchen, featuring French walnut cabinetry so perfectly matched that it appears honed from a single piece of wood.

The adjoining family room flows through to the more formal dining and living area, where 15-foot-high (4.5 m) ceilings maximize the sweeping views. "This would make a spectacular home for entertaining," says Wright. "You could easily host a couple of hundred guests. It's been designed with the highest level of easy living in mind." Sharing similar vistas, the master suite includes an office/yoga room as well as a see-through fireplace that looks onto the gardens. A junior master suite, two further bedrooms and baths, and a large game and media room complete the indoor family spaces.

Covered and uncovered terraces wrap around most of the residence, connecting the inside and outside areas, while the open-air kitchen and dining terrace, overlooking the pool and spa, invite alfresco entertaining. A separate wellness pavilion of 776 square feet (72 sq m) is a flexible space with kitchenette and bath that could alternatively be used as an unparalleled private home office. Further leisure amenities in the grounds include a sports court and putting green.

In addition, a luxurious, self-contained three-bedroom guesthouse is ideal for staff, benefiting from private access from the road, as well as its own lap pool. "It would make a wonderful home in itself," says Wright. "The hallway alone is spectacular, with an eye-level window running down its entire length, providing a panoramic view of the hills outside." »

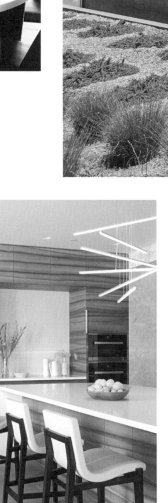

> "I've never seen a home that encapsulates indoor–outdoor living more graciously than this one... It's been designed with the highest level of easy living in mind." *Zackary Wright*

The finer things: Relish gourmet living in a kitchen crafted from French walnut and quartz countertops, complemented by Sub-Zero, Miele, and Wolf appliances. For dining under warm Californian skies, the expansive terrace is unbeatable.

Property
Whitehall Estate,
St. Helena, Napa
Valley, California, USA

Offered at
Price upon request

Contact
Zackary Wright
Christie's International
Real Estate
+1 310 385 2690
zwright@christies.com
christiesrealestate.com

A sense of place: From the sociable living areas to the tranquil bedrooms, and even the striking wine "cellar," walls of glass frame serene panoramas throughout the main home, anchoring it in its captivating setting.

Private oasis: Self-contained and superbly appointed, the three-bedroom, two-and-a-half-bath guesthouse has been lavished with high-quality finishes and amenities, including a honed lava-stone fireplace, outdoor grill, and lap pool.

"This would make a spectacular home for entertaining. You could easily host a couple of hundred guests." *Zackary Wright*

Destination: Napa Valley

CALIFORNIA DREAM

Famed for its outstanding wineries, restaurants, and scenery, Napa Valley has all the ingredients for a world-class lifestyle

Justifiably, Napa Valley is known the world over as a mecca for lovers of fine wine and gourmet food. The scenic 30-mile (48 km) stretch of northern California is home to more than 400 wineries and six Michelin-starred restaurants—10 if you include neighboring Sonoma County. All year round, visitors are drawn to this fertile, cultured region to sample exquisite produce, soak up the refined lifestyle, and drink in picture-perfect vistas of endless vineyards framed against backdrops of rolling hills and rugged mountains.

Just four miles (6.5 km) from Whitehall Estate is St. Helena. Nicknamed "Napa Valley's Main Street," it's the birthplace of the region's viticultural legacy and the area's most desirable small town, with charming shops, galleries, cafes, and eateries. Among the more recognizable wineries are Beringer and Louis M Martini, which happily coexist with boutique producers such as Vineyard 29 and Terra Valentine. Dining options include farm-to-table favorite The Charter Oak, while Thomas Keller's acclaimed The French Laundry—widely regarded as the dining experience of a lifetime—is less than 15 minutes' drive from the estate, in picturesque Yountville.

Also nearby is The Restaurant at Auberge du Soleil, in Rutherford. Napa's first fine-

Great pairing: Beringer's Rhine House veranda is an intimate setting for sampling the winery's offering (*top*), while The Charter Oak in St. Helena prides itself on seasonal fare that celebrates Napa Valley's bounty (*above*).

dining establishment opened its doors in 1981 and is today overseen by executive chef Robert Curry, who does amazing things with locally sourced seasonal ingredients. Book into one of the Auberge's suites so you can make the most of the sommelier's excellent wine suggestions.

Napa Valley's wine tourism gave rise to its famously good living, which offers a rich and varied leisure scene that's unmatched by other wine-growing regions around the world. Between wining and dining, work up an appetite and enjoy the scenery with excellent biking, hiking, and golfing. You can also take to the water at Lake Hennessey, to the east; the area's largest reservoir, it's perfect for fishing and boating. For an even more relaxed way of passing time, Calistoga, to the north, is a spa-seeker's haven, known for its mud baths and geothermal springs. The town also hosts a Saturday market showcasing produce from California's farms and ranches.

Connections to the region are superb, with flights into San Francisco, Oakland, or Sacramento airports, followed by a straightforward drive—around one hour and 40 minutes from any of them—or helicopter ride to Whitehall Estate itself. ●

EMILIO SÁNCHEZ (1921-1999)
Casa Vivienda
oil on canvas
24 × 36 in. (61 x 91.4 cm)
$20,000-25,000

LATIN AMERICAN ART
New York, 20-21 November 2019

VIEWING
16-20 November 2019
20 Rockefeller Plaza
New York, NY 10020

CONTACT
Virgilio Garza
vgarza@christies.com
+1 212 636 2150

CHRISTIE'S

For years you've loved the Hockney print that you bought at a charming New York gallery you visit whenever you are in town, and it still hangs in one of your guest rooms. But times change and, as you consider a change of decor, maybe it's time to pass it on to another collector.

But how do you go about selling a cherished work of art? How do you know how much it might be worth, and where might be the best place to sell it? As with most questions posed by 21st-century living, Google has some of the topline answers. See if any similar pieces are on the market, either at a gallery or at auction, and check their price tags. And see if an artist's "stock" is up or down in the art press. You could also buy a one-day pass to Artnet's Price Database for access to more than 12 million color art auction records dating back to 1985.

Jonathan Stone, Deputy Chairman of Asia and Co-Chairman of Asian Art at Christie's, recommends studying reports issued by major art fairs and institutions, such as Art Basel and Hiscox, "to have a better understanding of how the global market is performing." Stone also steers potential consignors (see box opposite) to christies.com, to check sale records in the category they wish to sell in.

PADDLE POWER

Last year, the world's leading auction houses sold more than $12 billion worth of art, with sales at Christie's accounting for more than half ($7 billion). "Selling at auction can maximize the outreach to a global client base and leverage extensive resources to best promote objects through global marketing, social media, preview tours, and art forums," says Stone.

Gemma Sudlow, Vice President, Specialist Head of Private & Iconic Collections, Christie's New York, adds: "At any given time of year we can find a suitable auction… Consigning your work to a gallery requires finding the right place for what you have and then, potentially, a considerable wait time with no guaranteed date of sale."

The first thing you need to do in order to become a consignor with Christie's

Words
STEVEN SHORT

Wondering how to go about putting that once-favorite piece up for sale? Our guide to selling your art at auction has everything you need to know

THAT'S YOUR LOT

is ascertain whether the house would be willing and able to sell your piece. You can either do this face to face, via appointment (you must supply a photo of the work first), or online by submitting up to three images and information about what you want to sell—the artist, medium, dimensions, and provenance, along with scans of any associated documentation you may have. Christie's experts will review your submission (free of charge) and come back to you with estimates within four to six weeks.

IT'S PERSONAL

The experts will then work with you to develop a personalized sales strategy. They'll explain the commission you will have to pay on a sale, and discuss the best way to sell—in the saleroom, via a private sale, or in an online auction. To attract millennial and emerging buyers, for example, an online-only auction might be best, while a private sale allows you to sell works outside of the auction calendar. A private sale also enables consignors to keep the sale low profile. It's worth noting that valuations can change once an expert has a piece in front of them. Try to give as much detail as possible when you send in the initial photographs.

Once you've signed a seller's agreement you will need to have your artwork delivered to a Christie's saleroom or warehouse. Christie's can arrange this for you, should you wish. The auction house will then photograph and catalog your property, and work out the best way to market it to potential buyers around the world. If you put your work in a public sale you may have to wait until a relevant sale comes up. Check christies.com for auction schedules.

"Items that are fresh to the market or have great provenance are the pieces that tend to exceed expectation. We specialize in ensuring that property is well-estimated, positioned well in the right sale context, and has creative marketing around it—that's why we achieve outstanding results for our vendors," observes Sudlow.

Before the sale, a specialist Christie's team reviews interest on the lot and agrees a reserve price with the seller.

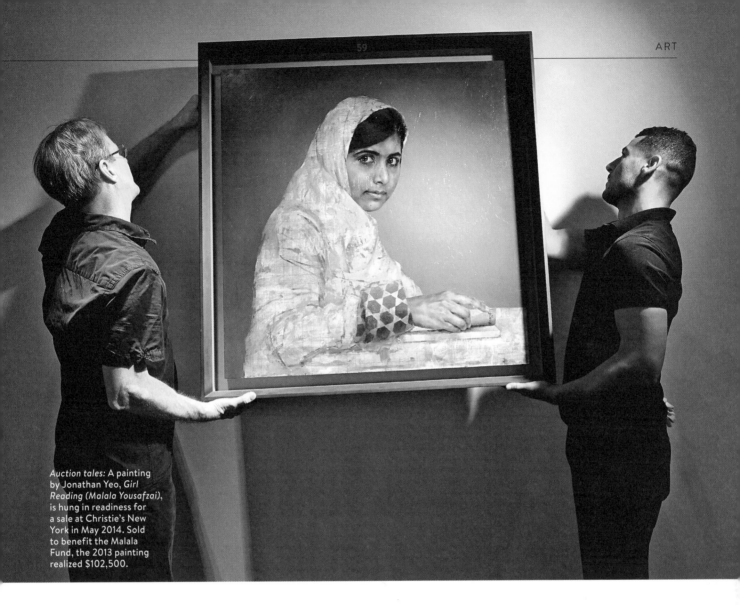

Auction tales: A painting by Jonathan Yeo, *Girl Reading (Malala Yousafzai)*, is hung in readiness for a sale at Christie's New York in May 2014. Sold to benefit the Malala Fund, the 2013 painting realized $102,500.

Many who sell art at a live auction like to attend the sale in person, though you can also watch remotely via Christie's LIVE. "An auction generates a sense of urgency and excitement in bidding that helps maximize the sale return to the seller," observes Stone. "It also ensures transparency while retaining the confidentiality of the seller and the buyer, unless they wish to be public."

After the sale you'll receive notification of how much your artwork finally sold for. The auction house will then confirm your net proceeds based on the hammer price, taking the seller's commission into account.

Christie's will then secure payment from the buyer, after which (typically around 35 days after the auction) your funds will be transferred to your nominated bank account, just in time for your next visit to New York, perhaps. ●

10 AUCTION TERMS TO KNOW

Consignor
The person who is selling property via the auction house.

Property
The item or group of items being put up for sale.

Provenance
A history of the item and how you acquired it.

Lot
An object or group of objects offered for sale as a single unit.

Reserve price
The confidential agreed minimum price. Your item will not be sold for less than this.

Bid
An offer on a lot from a potential buyer.

Fair warning
An indication that the hammer is about to come down on a lot.

Hammer price
The price at which the auctioneer's hammer falls, and at which he or she declares an item "sold."

Buyer's premium
The amount above the hammer price that must be paid as part of the total purchase price.

Seller's commission
A commission paid by the consignor to the auction house, which is deducted from the hammer price.

LET THERE BE LIGHT

As humans are naturally programmed to crave daylight, architects have developed new tricks to ensure that our homes are illuminated in the best possible way

Words **CLARE DOWDY**

Pity the villagers of Rjukan in Norway and Viganella in Italy, who until recently lived half the year in the shade as tall mountainsides blocked out their sunlight. But technology has come to their rescue—enormous mirrors have now been installed on nearby peaks to track the sun and reflect its rays into the deep valleys below. Their homes are dark no longer.

It's well known that a dearth of natural light brings with it a risk of developing seasonal affective disorder. Rjukan and Viganella may be in extreme locations, but natural light has health and well-being benefits wherever you are.

For architects as well as residents, there is an aesthetic upside to natural light. "It reveals the volumes in architecture, and conditions our perception of textures, materials, and colors," says architect Samuel Lamas of Equipe Lamas in Brazil.

There's also a green argument, as Kai Salmela of Salmela Architects in Duluth, Minnesota, explains. "Increased daylighting—combined with passive heating from the sun and passive ventilation from operable windows—can greatly reduce the energy costs and hence the environmental impacts of our buildings."

Traditionally, houses in many cooler parts of the world were built of solid stone or brick, both materials that historically make it hard to keep the heat in. To counter this, "People made the windows as small as possible," says architect Jane Burnside, who designs in Scotland and Ireland. "It wasn't about views."

Modern construction techniques, however, mean it's now possible to create big windows by spanning vast lengths across a lintel, with double- and triple-glazing keeping the heat in.

For architects with a love of light, there are a number of ways to draw it into homes, from ingenious apertures to clever layouts, thoughtful structure, and even kinetics. At the Cirqua Apartments complex in Melbourne, Australia, large, round windows work wonders. The development, by BKK Architects, stands on a steeply sloping site, and all the bedrooms and living areas of the 44 homes have direct access to natural light. »

Light fantastic: At Origami House in Northern Ireland —an award-winning design by Jane Burnside—angled walls of glass allow light to pour in, simultaneously framing discrete views of the garden and sky.

Seattle-based firm Olson Kundig takes this idea one step further in its three-story Treehouse on Costa Rica's Pacific coast. On the top and bottom floors, a double-layered teak screen, like slatted shutters, can be adjusted to create a solid or semi-open wall. When open, a play of light is allowed in. "It's almost like two fences on either side of a structure; one is shifted to open where the other is closed," says architect Tom Kundig.

The right light is, of course, dependent on orientation. At Equipe Lamas's Casa 28 in Brasília, big windows are mostly positioned east–west and the walls north–south. "This allows a dramatic natural light effect during sunrise and sunset, and gives open views across the house," says Lamas.

Poor orientation or low light levels can be alleviated by skylights. These, according to the Danish Building Research Institute, provide twice as much light as vertical windows and three times as much as dormers.

Burnside's own Origami House in Ballymena, Northern Ireland, faces west, meaning it doesn't get much light in winter. "We used long linear roof lights in the main living space to bring the south light in," she explains.

Meanwhile, in MSMR's compact townhouse on London's New Burlington Place, natural light is brought deep into the building by a top-lit sculptural stair.

QUANTITY AND QUALITY

"Every room should have a minimum of two sources of natural light, preferably three, and ideally four or even five," believes Salmela. His firm pulled this off in its hometown in Minnesota with the single-story Deloia House. Salmela describes it as one of the best examples the firm has of both quantity and quality of light. As well as narrow building widths and single-loaded corridors, the house has clerestory boxes (raised sections) in the ceiling that "act

CIRQUA APARTMENTS
Melbourne, Australia

This multi-residence development by BKK Architects features oversized porthole-style windows that channel natural light into all of the homes on the steeply sloping site. The articulated façade also reduces the building's mass at street level, and references the character of existing homes in the neighborhood.

"**Natural light reveals the volumes in architecture, and conditions our perception of textures, materials, and colors.**" *Samuel Lamas*

ORIGAMI HOUSE
Ballymena,
Northern Ireland

Inspired by Irish *clachans* (hamlets of cottages), Jane Burnside's Origami House—designed as her own family home—brings a contemporary vision to a traditional concept. Open-plan living spaces run throughout, walls of glass line the west façade, and linear roof lights draw in rays from the south.

almost like natural light chandeliers," according to the architect.

Skylights really come into their own with deep basements. Pilbrow & Partners top-lit a subterranean pool in a private house in Kensington, London, through five oculus portals. These support a shallow layer of water, which disperses natural light.

For a full-frontal blast of sunlight, the bigger the sliding door, the better. Modern technology means they can now be up to 33 feet (10 m) wide, and Polish firm KWK Promes put such doors to good use at Quadrant House. The client was after a home that would react to the sun's movement, so architect Rob Konieczny's solution was a static L-shaped building with a "wing" in between that pivots on tracks over the lawn. Meanwhile, Swiss window company Sky-Frame spent six months fashioning a bespoke motorized sliding system for the project, meaning the glazed living room can be completely open on two sides.

Clever consideration of layout and building structure can also increase natural light, as MSMR's townhouse demonstrates. Occupying just 1,292 square feet (120 sq m), the home is squeezed onto a former garage site between London's Regent Street and Savile Row. It's landlocked on three sides, so the building's »

TREEHOUSE
Santa Teresa, Costa Rica

Set amid thick forest, the Treehouse (*pictured above*) by Olson Kundig architects is characterized by two floors that are open to the elements, with daylight, airflow, and privacy controlled by slatted teak screens. The Treehouse "breathes and embraces the local climate," says Tom Kundig.

CASA 28
Brasília, Brazil

The generous 1.7-acre (0.7 ha) site enabled Casa 28 (*pictured right and below*) to be precisely positioned for optimum natural light and views. The inclusion of tilting windows allows cross-ventilation in every room.

DELOIA HOUSE
Duluth, Minnesota

At this single-story residence by Salmela Architects, cubic skylight structures extend from above the roofline down into the interior volume. "The boxes reflect natural light down into the space, with openings that disperse the light in all directions," explains Kai Salmela.

Modern masterpiece
Park City, Utah, USA
$14,000,000
Windermere Real Estate-Utah
Daimon Bushi
+1 435 200 4959
With direct ski access from its own ski-prep room, this 12,303 sq ft (1,143 sq m) contemporary residence is located within the elite ski community of The Colony at White Pine Canyon and offers unrivaled privacy. Highlights of the 4.5-acre (1.82 ha) estate include a master wing accessed via a skywalk over a stream, expansive heated decks, and a chef's kitchen with attached caterer's kitchen.

The Dream
Platinum Coast, Barbados
Price upon request
One Caribbean Estates
Chris Parra
+1 246 826 4252
Located in The Garden, an exclusive neighborhood, this five-bedroom home features contemporary ultramodern design and a focus on indoor–outdoor living. Landscaped gardens surround covered terraces, a large sundeck, an infinity-edge pool and an outdoor barbecue lounge area, while the beautiful interiors blend seamlessly with the modern look and showcase clean lines, cool neutral hues, and tropical indulgence.

street-facing façade needed to provide all the light and air to the habitable rooms, without compromising privacy. The architects' solution was to put the main rooms at the front of the house, and push the ancillary accommodation to the back. And by stepping back the front elevation, the basement gets access to daylight.

Letting the light in is not entirely without its drawbacks. In northern Europe, Burnside warns about overheating. "It depends on the building system. Origami House has a heavy mass to absorb excess heat and lets it out slowly. In a timber-framed house, you don't have a heavy mass inside, only the floor to absorb the heat."

Meanwhile, in the southern hemisphere, to get better lighting throughout the year (with greater thermal comfort in winter) the openings should be oriented to the south, and the design should avoid problems of direct sunlight, explains Lamas. For extremely hot climates, with short winters, it's better to have a combination of north and south openings.

Salmela says the goal isn't necessarily to maximize light, "but to achieve the right quantity and quality of light for the space and function." He cautions that "too much direct light can be a problem, causing excessive glare and heat gain, and UV damage to materials." Deloia House counters this with a thin, cantilevered flat roof that gives some shade to the windows during the hottest parts of the day in high summer. Other features that can be used to keep out strong rays and prevent overheating are *brise-soleil*, pergolas, and balconies.

And as the inhabitants of any heavily glazed building know—including those of London's Neo Bankside, which stands right next to Tate Modern—windows allow views in as well as out. As Salmela puts it: "The level of transparency or privacy is both an individual preference and a cultural consideration." ●

Clare Dowdy writes about architecture and design for Wallpaper*, Monocle, *and* The Guardian, *and is editor of* Furnace *magazine*

COREY GAFFER

Yanick Delafoge, also known as Yanidel, was in the Paris Métro one afternoon when he spotted two lovers. "I had a second to lift the camera, compose, and press the shutter," he recalls of capturing *The Republic of Love*, a moment of intimacy framed within the doors of a train in a station full of strangers.

Some street photographers see themselves as fishermen, finding their perfect setting and composition and patiently waiting for their subject to appear, while others describe their approach as hunting, always on the move, chasing what the pioneer of the genre, Henri Cartier-Bresson, called "the decisive moment"; when all the elements of the image come together in an instant.

Yanidel is definitely in that latter category. "I'm not a very patient person. I keep on moving and react to opportunities as they cross my path. Many of my pictures are taken in a split second and I rarely have time to take more than one or two shots. By experience, the first shot is often the best since it is usually completely intuitive," says the Swiss photographer, now based in Argentina.

London's Ronya Galka could also be described as a hunter. "I roam the street for hours on end in search of moments to capture and memories to make." Noting that every photographer has their own style and approach in order to stay unnoticed and unobserved, she points out that she likes to "move with the flow of the city. There is life to be observed everywhere, and standing in one place for an extended period feels like I am limiting myself too much."

Street photography became a genre in its own right in the early 1930s when technological advancements in handheld cameras made them easily transportable, more user-friendly, and appropriately discreet. The compact Leica, with its superior lens quality, became the camera of choice for many of history's street photography masters such as Cartier-Bresson, Elliott Erwitt, »

City view: Alan Schaller's *Tate, London,* part of his *Metropolis* series, examines how we are dwarfed by the modern world around us, and often lost within it.

IN THE BLINK OF AN EYE

By capturing a moment that others might never be aware of, street photographers can make us look at the world around us from a new perspective. We meet the best practitioners working today

Words **SONIA KOLESNIKOV-JESSOP**

Robert Frank, Ilse Bing, and Garry Winogrand, helping them elevate their work into an art form.

"When street photography matured during the early- to mid-20th century, it stood out from earlier photographic practices in that the images were no longer staged and no longer printed using painterly techniques in order to justify their status as fine art," explains Rebecca Jones, Junior Specialist, Photographs at Christie's New York. "The candid nature of street photographs, and the speed of their making, is very much a part of the modern art movement of photography," she adds.

For Jones, street photography is "the artistic practice of reflexively composing images in the camera," while embedded in a particular locale in order to capture its character. "Skilled street photography will result in precise compositions, in which every element of form and expression is integral, and nothing is superfluous," she says.

"Street photography demands vision, discipline, technique, and an ability to translate a message to a viewer. These are all hallmark aspects of most art forms," remarks Alan Schaller, a London-based photographer who in 2015 cofounded the

YANIDEL

Working in the moment, Yanidel captures the coincidences, poetry, and humor of daily life. A lyrical, storytelling quality runs through his images, evident in the likes of *Shattered Dream* (*above right*), *A Reflection of Lovers* (*top left*), and *Lady in Phone Booth* (*above left*).

Street Photography International collective to promote the best of the genre from around the world, notably via its Instagram account, which now has some 970,000 followers.

While street photography is often associated with documentary photography, and both capture candid moments, the two genres are actually quite different, as New York-based Matthew Pillsbury explains: "With street photography you are telling a story… making a fiction out of elements found in the real world. Documentary photography should have an obligation to be more accurate in the way it presents itself. It's meant to be a reporting of the real."

"Street photography allows me as the photographer to record and share the mystery of life, the unexpected side of reality that is constantly taking me by surprise," says Galka, adding that she shoots with her heart, following her instincts. "For me the act of photographing in the street is a highly subjective process. I don't necessarily show things as they are but how I see them. It's that ambiguity that makes this genre of photography so interesting and artful." »

RONYA GALKA

In shots such as *Mates* (*left*) and *Those Who Don't Believe in Magic Will Never Find It* (*below*), Galka celebrates the surprises that permeate everyday life, from the "pure, innocent joy" of seemingly mundane situations to "wonderfully random" chance encounters.

ALAN SCHALLER

Discipline and technique are key to Schaller's work—which includes *London Underground* (*left*) and *British Museum, London* (*above*)—but instinct plays a role too. *Pigeon Served Three Ways* (*top*) "came about after 10 minutes of waiting. I was aiming for the reflection of the bird in the window... the shadow was a surprise."

Good instincts and chance play an important role in the art form. "In the age of cell phones, people don't seem to look at their surroundings anymore. Yet, humor, poetry, coincidences are all over, for the ones who look for them," remarks Yanidel, pointing out that chance is also directly correlated with time spent hunting in the streets.

"Chance is always an element, but I rarely depend entirely on it," adds Schaller. "Sometimes a moment will just materialize, but I find the technique is in understanding the potential of a scene and what realistically can happen. Having a goal when shooting a scene helps me know when it has been achieved or not. It's good to have an idea of what you want, but you shouldn't be blinkered."

While Schaller and Galka shoot in black and white—"black and white allows photographers to strip away any distractions and focus the viewers' eyes on what they want them to see," remarks Galka—others play on color to channel certain moods in their visual storytelling.

Liam Wong uses a neon-noir cyberpunk aesthetic, inspired by the cinematographic work of Wong Kar-wai, Gaspar Noé, and Ridley Scott, to immortalize Tokyo nightlife. "I like to capture real moments and turn them into the surreal," the photographer explains, adding that he tends to focus on architecture and silhouettes, not faces.

"I love how graphic principles, color, content, and composition all play their part in creating a mood. In some cases I barely edit the image, often shooting with a cooler white balance. Other times I will completely change the colors to create the mood I am going for," he explains. And though he does love spontaneous street photography, Wong also plans his shoots: "I will often mark interesting locations on a map to return to them at a later date. Sometimes I will lock on a location and wait for something interesting to present itself.

"I usually have a clear idea of the image I wish to create as I am taking the picture. As I'm naturally drawn towards composition, it gives »

MATTHEW PILLSBURY

The long exposures used by Pillsbury encourage viewers to appreciate the transient nature of life. *Clockwise from top left: Sandcastle Competition; Haname #12; Edgewater Beach #3; Goya's Last Communion of St Joseph.*

me clear rules as to where I can position myself to get the right shot," he explains. Wong's debut monograph *TO:KY:OO* is about to be published by Thames & Hudson.

Pillsbury's distinctive work, defined by long exposures of anywhere from 20 seconds to an hour, underlines that street photography today extends behind the handheld camera. "In using longer exposures I hope to make viewers look at our world with a renewed sense of discovery. I invite people to think about the evanescent or transient nature of our existence and how we make use of the spaces we occupy. I love this idea of the city providing us these stages upon which the dramas of our lives take place," he remarks.

In recent years, image-sharing sites such as Instagram, Flickr, and Tumblr have increased interest in street photography. "By its very nature, street photography represents one of the most democratic art forms of the photography genres," says Galka. "And with the advent of affordable cameras and smartphones, more people are capturing the life around them. For many people, street photography provides an entry point into

LIAM WONG

Radiating a neon-noir aesthetic, Wong's work draws inspiration from cinematography, sci-fi, and Japanese animation. *Clockwise from top left: Midgar Nights* nods to Japanese sci-fi franchise *Final Fantasy; Memories of Green* pays homage to Ridley Scott's *Blade Runner* (1982); *Tokyo Night Train.*

photography overall, then often flows into other genres such as portrait, documentary, and travel."

The market for street photography is booming. At auction, images by Cartier-Bresson can expect to achieve $10,000–$30,000, Jones says, adding: "The same is generally true of Robert Frank, though the market prefers the more rare, vintage photographs, which can achieve more than $100,000. The record for one of Frank's photographs is $663,750, achieved for *Trolley, New Orleans, 1955* at Christie's New York in 2013."

Works by Diane Arbus can also achieve high figures (in 2018, *Identical Twins, Roselle, N.J., 1966* sold for $732,500 at Christie's New York), while dye-transfer prints by William Eggleston also have the potential to exceed $300,000, Jones remarks.

And it's not just the big names attracting the interest of collectors. As Jones observes: "There is notable enthusiasm for the younger generation of photographers practicing street photography, or offshoots from this classic genre." ●

Sonia Kolesnikov-Jessop is an arts and lifestyle journalist who writes for Robb Report Singapore, CNN, *and* The New York Times International Edition

A RARE PAIR OF IMPERIAL EMBELLISHED LAPIS LAZULI 'DA JI' DOUBLE-GOURD-FORM PLAQUES
QIANLONG PERIOD (1736-1795)
19 in. (48.2 cm.) high overall including wood stands inset with hardstones, gilt-bronze and stained ivory
£120,000-180,000

**FINE CHINESE CERAMICS
AND WORKS OF ART**

London, 5 November 2019

VIEWING
1-4 November
8 King Street
London SW1Y 6QT

CONTACT
Kate Hunt
khunt@christies.com
+44 (0)207 752 3389

PALAZZO PERFECTION

Beautiful outside, incredible inside, this villa is rich in history and design credentials alike

Words **AILEEN SCOULAR**

Within these walls: Set in the small, characterful town of Cetona, the imposing Villa La Vagnola is a rare Tuscan estate, with generous proportions, fairytale grounds, and incredible interiors.

"Renzo Mongiardino roamed the globe for a cornucopia of colors, finishes, and artifacts."

For two decades, a striking 18th-century villa on a travertine-tiled square in the sleepy Tuscan town of Cetona has offered its residents a wonderful escape from the pressures of life. Villa La Vagnola's lush Italianate gardens offer a cocoon from the outside world, while its sumptuous interiors deliver an escape of an altogether different kind.

This is an Italian villa like no other. Its mellow sun-drenched walls and pretty shuttered windows may mirror the pastel-colored architecture spiraling up the hill towards Cetona's medieval fortress, but the interior was reimagined in the late 1980s by one of Europe's most influential designers, Renzo Mongiardino. When the owner commissioned Mongiardino to transform his new home, he could not have imagined the realms of fantasy and invention that his architect would reach.

Having himself grown up in an impressive 18th-century palazzo in Genoa, Mongiardino understood the villa's spirit and redecorated accordingly. Taking a series of early 19th-century watercolor paintings as his inspiration, and harnessing his expertise in theater and film design, he roamed the globe for a cornucopia of colors, finishes, and artifacts. Venetian cabinetry, Byzantine wallcoverings, and Oriental statuary were combined with allegorical ceilings and *trompe l'oeil* wall paintings.

OUT OF THIS WORLD
Such is the intricate level of detail throughout the villa that it is impossible to highlight one room over another, although the majestic painted ceiling in the billiards room certainly elevates this humble game to the sport of kings, and the terracotta- and marble-tiled floors are almost too beautiful to tread upon.

Thirty years after renovations began, the villa's glorious interior remains intact, matched by its generous proportions: 17,216 square feet (1,600 sq m), with 15 bedrooms and 12 baths. "The property is a typical Tuscan *villa padronale* but its size makes it unusual," notes Riccardo Romolini of Agenzia Romolini Immobiliare Srl, the exclusive affiliate of Christie's »

International Real Estate in the region. "Around Cetona, luxury farmhouses are probably the most common piece of real estate, whereas this villa feels more like a historic palazzo in Florence."

The 27-acre (11 ha) estate is also extensive, containing leafy parkland and an olive grove, alongside Italianate gardens. Here again, only the best was commissioned, including the expertise of landscape architect Paolo Pejrone, who sculpted the garden into a series of rooms and terraces to provide privacy and shade. Like Mongiardino, Pejrone was a familiar face in European society, and he studied under legendary English garden designer Russell Page and Brazilian artist Roberto Burle Marx. "By dividing the garden into different themed areas, you always experience the same feelings of privacy and intimacy that you enjoy inside the villa," says Romolini. "The flowers and trees are also typical of the Italian garden: holm oak, cypress, maple, boxwood, yew, plus citrus fruits, roses, and hydrangeas."

GARDEN OF DELIGHTS

The grounds yield some surprises, too. There is a 200-seat stone amphitheater and a genuine Etruscan tomb dating back to the 7th century BC. The winter garden is veiled in creeper, and houses an orangery and a gym. And one of the property's original buildings, La Turkerie, today overlooks an inviting pool: built in 1837 to celebrate a visiting Turkish pasha, the conical building is now a pool pavilion, with extravagant frescos.

Even the ground beneath Villa La Vagnola conceals its own secrets. The villa was built in 1750 to celebrate the wedding of local nobleman Salustio Terrosi and his bride Maria Antonietta Vagnoli, and Terrosi stipulated a labyrinth of underground tunnels. In the past, these chambers have been used to produce and store wine and there is ample opportunity to reignite the property's vinological heritage: Cetona's climate and geography is perfectly suited to growing vines and olives. "The amount of land would make it possible to establish a new wine estate, or to create a relaxing spa retreat," agrees Romolini.

Indeed, for all its country charm, Cetona is well-connected. "Although located in Tuscany, it's very close to the borders of Umbria and Latium so it's easy to reach Siena, Florence, and Rome," notes Romolini. "The small town is full of character. And with wine production becoming one of the main activities of this region, there's growing appeal for international residents."

Today, Villa La Vagnola may no longer resemble the marital home that Terrosi once created but, thanks to Mongiardino's painterly vision and Pejrone's harmonious aesthetic, it remains rich in romance of an entirely different kind. ●

Room with a view: Designer Renzo Mongiardino commissioned the bohemian glass-walled garden room (*above and top right*) to link his Baroque-style interiors to the gardens beyond, where landscape architect Paolo Pejrone introduced themed "rooms" and layers of lush green foliage.

Property
Villa La Vagnola, Cetona,
Tuscany, Italy

Offered at
€12,000,000

Contacts
Riccardo Romolini
Agenzia Romolini Immobiliare Srl
+39 0575 788 948
info@romolini.com
romolini.com

Charlotte Delaney
Christie's International
Real Estate
+44 20 7389 2551
cdelaney@christies.com
christiesrealestate.com

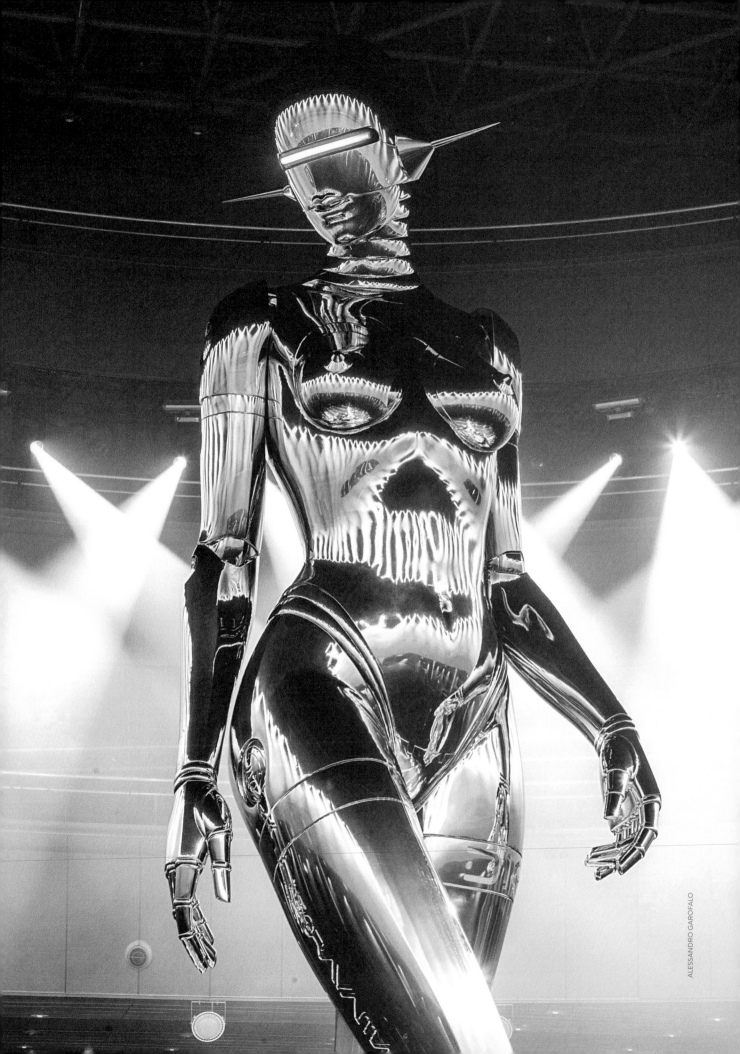

THE ART OF FASHION

Ever since Elsa Schiaparelli and Salvador Dalí's famous lobster dress, fashion designers and artists have pooled their creativity. We take a look at art and fashion's enduring love affair

Words **DAVID WATERS**

A fashion designer needs to be a voracious collector and hoarder of ideas, with a magpie's roving eye. He or she can take inspiration from pretty much anything—from a butterfly's wing to a tornado; from an Egyptian goddess to a political placard at a demonstration. Yet what gets fashion designers' creative juices flowing more than anything is the dazzle and visual punch of art.

When he was creative director of Louis Vuitton, Marc Jacobs once opened a fashion show with 12 models, among them Naomi Campbell, dressed as the subjects of Richard Prince's *Nurses* paintings, right down to their medical masks. Each woman carried a Vuitton monogrammed handbag printed with text from Prince's *Monochromatic Jokes* painting series. What were the gathered fashion editors watching? Was this a copy of Prince's work, an extension, or an homage?

In our visually saturated world, fashion and art "brands" can mutually benefit from such creative bonding. For the artist it's the crossover exposure and online reach, while the designer is temporarily bathed in the gravitas of the artist's high-culture aura. It often feels like a win, win.

"If you have a good eye, whatever you do in collaboration looks exciting," says Simon Costin, the set designer who famously worked with Alexander McQueen on his most groundbreaking early fashion shows. Yet according to Costin, the fashion and art worlds are distinct. "I was once

Metal master: Hajime Sorayama's robot was the Insta-hit of Kim Jones's pre-Fall 2019 menswear show for Dior Homme.

asked if Alexander McQueen was a true artist. I said, no, he was a genius fashion designer. And that's enough. Fine art functions in a very different way—it moves much slower. Whereas fashion is instant and is all about now."

McQueen's is the name most linked to the designer-as-artist idea. In a show called *Voss*, he recreated a disturbing image by the American artist Joel-Peter Witkin, *Sanitarium* (1983). Presented in a one-way mirrored box like a padded asylum, the presentation climaxed with a naked reclining woman wearing a winged face mask connected to a breathing device as large, papery moths flew around her.

SEAMLESS CONNECTION

Surely this was more performance art than fashion show? It was precisely this kind of ambiguity that gave many of McQueen's fashion shows their startling visceral impact. "A truly shocking, enthralling tableau," reported *Vogue* magazine when the lights had dimmed.

"I grew up watching McQueen's incredible shows," says Stephan Alexander, director of the Ghost Gallery in Brooklyn and Los Angeles. "In many ways they inspired me to do what I do now." It's the visual spectacles that lead Alexander to see fashion and art as seamlessly linked. "Technology is driving the connection between fashion and art more than anything else," he says. "Instagram has moved things on the most. It helps fashion »

Graphic scene: Alexander McQueen's *Voss* show featured a feather-clad model in a headpiece made out of stuffed hawks.

"Alexander McQueen was a genius fashion designer. And that's enough. Fine art functions in a very different way."
Simon Costin

Fine art: Marc Jacobs was inspired by Richard Prince's *Nurses* paintings for one catwalk show (*left*), while Raf Simons has repurposed prints by artist Sterling Ruby on silk dress fabric (*above*).

CANVAS TO CATWALK

In 1965, **Yves Saint Laurent** paid homage to **Mondrian** with a series of cocktail dresses inspired by the artist's stark, linear works. The A-line dresses were made using heavy fabrics, ensuring no distraction from the designs.

Salvador Dalí worked with designer **Elsa Schiaparelli** on several high-fashion creations. As well as an attention-grabbing hat in the shape of a shoe, the Spaniard collaborated on a dress with a lobster print—for Dalí the crustacean represented sexuality.

For her Spring 2018 show **Miuccia Prada** worked with eight female illustrators noted for representations of strong women. The comic-book-inspired show featured the work of **Brigid Elva** (above) and **Fiona Staples**.

designers and artists check in on each other's work as smoothly as scrolling through text—everything is delivered so fast now."

Andrew Bolton, chief curator of the Metropolitan Museum of Art's Costume Institute, isn't one to trouble himself over the difference between art and fashion either. "The art world sees fashion as something that is deeply rooted in the commercial world, not in the art world," he said in a recent interview. "And the popularity of fashion can be annoying to some people—they don't like that it brings in such huge numbers. But the reason why it does is that it's a living art form we can all relate to."

CELEBRITY FOCUS
The extravagant, celeb-drenched Met Gala launches Bolton's annual themed show. By drawing such large fee-paying crowds it is an important contributor to the Met Museum's bottom line. For instance, the 2015 show, *China: Through the Looking Glass*, raised $12.5 million and drew crowds of more than 800,000 to the museum in the four months the exhibition ran. The Met may be a museum of high art and design, but the commercial clout of fashion will never worry the museum's accountants.

Sometimes an artist's work subtly inspires a fashion collection. When Belgian minimalist

designer Raf Simons created his first couture collection for Christian Dior he repurposed the paintings of his friend, the artist and former skateboarder Sterling Ruby. These were copied onto silk to make dresses and skirts that glowed with streaks of the artist's rich, painterly color.

Simons and Ruby collaborated again when the designer took over Calvin Klein as creative director in 2016. Simons asked Ruby to overhaul the brand's minimalist Madison Avenue flagship store designed by British architect John Pawson. Given a free rein, the artist painted every surface acid yellow and installed scaffolding on which to hang the collection. It was a radical departure from Calvin Klein's low-key neutral palette. "I want the new store to glow from within," said Ruby, "representing a new day for Calvin Klein."

Surprisingly, however, their collaboration didn't pay off. Simons's contract with Calvin Klein ended abruptly at the end of 2018, when the label's owner decided to stop presenting catwalk collections altogether to focus on jeans, underwear, and fragrance.

Fashion commentators like Vanessa Friedman, chief fashion critic of *The New York Times*, felt Simons had turned this quintessential American label into something too high-concept. Too artsy, in fact. The lesson seems to be that if a designer becomes overly enthralled with art they risk »

On the market
FASHION CITY GEMS

Elegant grandeur
Paris, France
Price upon request
Daniel Féau Conseil
Immobilier
Marie-Hélène Lundgreen
+33 6 60 34 14 62
This reception apartment,
meticulously decorated
in 18th-century style by
interior designer Jacques
Garcia, is located in the
8th district. An entrance
hall leads to a suite of
paneled reception rooms
with soaring ceilings, which
open onto a private garden
and two bedroom suites.
The resplendent master
suite with walk-in closet and
spacious bath also opens
onto the formal garden.

Dramatic penthouse
London, UK
£8,200,000
Strutt & Parker
London New Homes
+44 20 7338 4677
Situated in the iconic
former home of British
broadcasting, Television
Centre, this four-bedroom,
four-bath penthouse was
designed by Stirling Prize
winner Allford Hall
Monaghan Morris and is
flooded with natural light.
Residents have access to
London's largest private
gym, swimming pool, sauna,
steam room, and hammam,
as well as a private lounge,
a screening room, and a
24-hour concierge.

Wide influence: Figures of Speech, the Virgil Abloh retrospective (*above*), and the Sterling Ruby-designed Calvin Klein store (*right*).

losing sight of the grueling commercial demands of the six-month fashion cycle.

This is an accusation that is unlikely ever to be leveled at one of the biggest names in men's fashion right now: Kim Jones, artistic director at Dior Homme (and former artistic director of menswear at Louis Vuitton) who likes nothing more than to work with artists. Jones showed his pre-Fall 2019 menswear presentation in Tokyo where he commissioned the Japanese sculptor Hajime Sorayama to make a towering, 39-foot (12 m), buxom aluminum robot woman who stood center stage as his sport-luxe attired models marched around her like minions.

Meanwhile, Virgil Abloh, men's artistic director at Louis Vuitton, has side-stepped the issue by blurring the lines between artist and designer completely. With more than 4 million Instagram followers and the ability to move smoothly between design, fashion, and club

culture, Abloh is as much a brand himself as any company he works with. He has his own fashion label Off-White; he has designed rugs for IKEA and he DJs in the best nightclubs. He has even designed record covers for Kanye West.

It should come as no surprise then that this summer Abloh's work was given a retrospective at the Museum of Contemporary Art Chicago called *Figures of Speech*. "Virgil is the type of creator who would devour everything around him and turn it into his nourishment," Japanese artist Takashi Murakami once said, defending the right of a designer to have his work displayed in a museum of art. When we are all magpies absorbing images at breakneck speed, Abloh is a perfect embodiment of the artist/designer for our digital age. ●

David Waters is a style and design writer who has contributed to The Telegraph, FT, GQ *and the* New York Observer

TENNIS.
ALL YEAR
LONG.

WATCH
AUSTRALIAN
OPEN
LIVE

JAN 20–
FEB 02

SWING INTO SPRING
Jan 29 — April 6

ROAD TO ROLAND GARROS
April 7 — June 10

LONDON CALLING
Jun 11 — Jul 15

SUMMER IN THE CITIES
Jul 16 — Sept 9

CHASE FOR THE CHAMPIONSHIPS
Sept 10 — Nov 18

HOME FOR THE HOLIDAYS
Nov 19 — Dec 30

SUMMER DOWN UNDER
Dec 31 — Jan 28

**And don't miss the best on-air team
in the business**

DOWNLOAD
THE APP TODAY!

DIRECTV (ch. 217),
DISH (ch. 400) or your
local tv provider!

TENNIS
C H A N N E L

Modern elegance

Jupiter Island, Florida, USA
This architectural gem is distinguished by exceptional design elements that maximize the appeal of its stunning oceanfront location. A wide foyer leads to a large light-filled loggia, which can be used to great effect as an art gallery, while a split plan features three bedrooms and four baths connected by a breathtaking living room and dining area that overlooks 175 ft (53 m) of scenic beachfront. The luxurious master suite features dual baths, a spa, and ocean views, and the estate is completed by a private patio area, a pool and spa, and a two-vehicle garage.
$7,650,000
Fenton & Lang
Joanne Wagner
+1 561 373 3127

ARTISTIC LICENSE

These four exceptional properties reveal how imaginative design can elevate a living space, and all are for sale through our global network of exclusive affiliates

Splendid isolation

Biarritz, France
Surrounded by private wooded grounds, this contemporary villa offers wonderful views through its many floor-to-ceiling windows. The first floor comprises a large and light living space, generous open-plan kitchen, and dining area that overlook the property's terrace and pool. Upstairs are six bedrooms, including a master suite that opens onto a terrace with enchanting views of the garden, as well as five baths and a spacious glass-walled room that would be perfect as an artist's studio. Outside, the grand pool house also features a studio space.
$4,262,332
Côte Ouest Immobilier
Audrey Durand
+33 5 59 26 82 60

Royal appointment

Perugia, Umbria, Italy
Nobleman Romeo Gallenga expanded
this charming residence in 1880, enlisting
architect Nazareno Biscarini to realize his
dream of creating a neo-Gothic castle.
Today, this remarkable property spans
35 rooms over five floors, which add up
to 29,062 sq ft (2,700 sq m) of palatial
architecture and opulent living spaces,
along with some 8,611 sq ft (800 sq m)
of stables and outbuildings. The structure
is crowned by an octagonal tower with
a marvellous rooftop terrace, offering
360-degree views over the rolling hills
and verdant countryside.
Price upon request
Agenzia Romolini Immobiliare Srl
Riccardo Romolini
+39 0575 788948

Ocean escape

Lahaina, Hawaii, USA
Built by globally renowned maritime artist
Christian Riese Lassen, this West Maui
residence is the ultimate in contemporary
design. Every detail of the 7,800 sq ft
(725 sq m) five-bedroom property has
been skillfully crafted, from the grand hall
living area highlighted by tall motorized
glass pocket doors that open onto an
idyllic private beachfront, to the infinity-
edge pool and integrated rock waterfall.
Other features include an expansive
lounge with office, oceanfront dining
area, gym, media room, elevator, two hot
tubs, outdoor grill station, and wet bar.
$13,500,000
Hawaii Life Real Estate Brokers
Jeff Onderko
+1 808 280 4881

FAST COMPANY

The synergy between art and Christie's International Real Estate ensured that a rare NYC listing sold in just 32 days

Even the most desirable home can take some time to sell. Seasonality, changing market conditions, and local and global events can all slow progress. That was the case with a West Village triplex that had been on the market with various realtors before Erin Boisson Aries, principal of the Erin Boisson Aries Team at Christie's International Real Estate Group in New York City, stepped in. "The seller is a valued customer of Christie's auction house," says Boisson Aries, "so it was essential that the client receive the same level of discretion and attention from our team at Christie's International Real Estate as they would from Christie's, and that we ultimately would be successful in selling their property."

The triplex, located in the heart of New York's West Village, was constructed for showcasing art and offers 9,600 square feet (892 sq m) of living space. With Boisson Aries's understanding of how to price and market such a rare listing, the apartment at the Abingdon (320 West 12th Street) sold for $30 million in just 32 days, making it the quickest—and most expensive—resale of 2019 when it sold in May.

"This experience was a reminder of the strength of the Christie's brand and the power of client relationships in continuing to build and expand our business," says Boisson Aries.

ON THE MARKET

Presenting more than 160 exceptional
properties in the world's most
spectacular locations

CHRISTIE'S
INTERNATIONAL REAL ESTATE

2019 AUCTION DATES

Christie's is pleased to announce the following
dates for our 2019 auction calendar.

If you would like a complimentary valuation for potential
inclusion in a sale, please contact a member of the department.

19TH CENTURY RUBY AND
DIAMOND NECKLACE
THE PROPERTY OF A EUROPEAN FAMILY
CHF 350,000-550,000
Magnificent Jewels,
Geneva, 12 November 2019

MAGNIFICENT JEWELS
Geneva, 12 November 2019

CONTACT
Jean-Marc Lunel
jlunel@christies.com
+41 (0) 22 319 1730

MAGNIFICENT JEWELS
Hong Kong, 26 November 2019

CONTACT
Vickie Sek
vsek@christies.com
+852 2978 9922

IMPORTANT JEWELS
London, 27 November 2019

CONTACT
Keith Penton
kpenton@christies.com
+44 (0) 20 7389 2526

MAGNIFICENT JEWELS
New York, 11 December 2019

CONTACT
Daphne Lingon
dlingon@christies.com
+1 212 636 2300

JEWELS
Paris, 5 December 2019

CONTACT
Violane d'Astorg
vdastorg@christies.com
+33 1 40 76 85 81

CHRISTIE'S

EUROPE & AFRICA

Pages 91-125

SERENE RADIANCE
WÄHRING, VIENNA

- **Close to shops and restaurants**
- **Lush gardens with a swimming pool**
- **Beautifully finished interiors**

Nestled in its own oasis, this resplendent villa exceeds all expectations, combining a highly desirable location with a sensational interior living space. On the first floor, a grand entrance with cloakroom leads to the bright open-plan living and dining room with adjoining kitchen, while a vast, light-flooded conservatory opens straight out to the stunning terrace for easy indoor–outdoor living. On the upper floor, a large anteroom leads to three bedrooms—one of which has direct access to a second terrace with garden views. Abundant accommodation is provided by a further four bedrooms in the attic, in addition to two baths, a sauna, and a centrally accessible kitchen, while undeveloped space on this level offers a number of options. Outside, south-facing verandas overlook a shimmering swimming pool and lush grounds that include a potential building lot. A fitness room, wine cellar, storage space, and two-car garage complete this prestigious home.

OFFERED AT Price upon request
INQUIRIES **Avantgarde Properties**,
avantgardeproperties.com
ASSOCIATE Elisabeth Karoly,
office@avantgardeproperties.com,
+43 664 115 1775
ON THE WEB Search for C59908

MAGNIFICENT VIEWS
LAKE DISTRICT, SALZBURG

- **25 minutes from Salzburg city center**
- **Finished to exacting standards**
- **More than 1.7 acres (0.7 ha) with lush gardens**

Nestled in an elevated position with marvelous panoramic views, this sublime eight-bedroom, eight-bath villa, in a quiet area surrounded by rolling countryside, is a rare find in Salzburg. Built in 2005, the timeless piece of architecture gently combines the warmth and comfort of an Austrian chalet with the elegance of a stately

home. An ornately carved front door opens to more than 7,700 sq ft (715 sq m) of beautifully finished living space, complete with an elevator to all floors. A manicured garden matches the extremely high standards of the house. With all the main lake and skiing areas close by, this family dwelling is perfectly located and has 360-degree vistas stretching all the way from Lake Mondsee to the mountains surrounding Salzburg. The country's principal motorway is just a 10-minute drive away, giving easy access to shopping, fine dining, and other amenities, and the residence is also less than 30 minutes from the city's international airport.

OFFERED AT €3,850,000
INQUIRIES **Stiller & Hohla Immobilientreuhänder GmbH**, stiller-hohla.at
ASSOCIATE Dr Berndt Kretschmer, buy@stiller-hohla.at, +43 662 6585 110
ON THE WEB Search for C58305

V TOWER PENTHOUSE
PRAGUE

- **Four bedrooms and four full baths**
- **Rooftop terrace with swimming pool**
- **Five-star residents' amenities**

The largest apartment in the striking 30-floor V Tower, Prague—a new icon of the capital's skyline—this exclusive penthouse offers a generous 9,321 sq ft (866 sq m) of indoor and outdoor living space. Spanning three levels, including a rooftop terrace with a swimming pool, the property boasts beautiful 360-degree views of the city and a high-tech 4,843 sq ft (450 sq m) interior with an elevator to all floors, a cutting-edge cooling and heating system, and acoustic insulation for ultimate privacy. Each of the four bedrooms has its own bath, as well as access to a balcony or the fully glazed main terrace—itself an exceptional setting for entertaining, with the city lights providing a glittering backdrop at night. The tower's residents benefit from five-star hotel-style amenities, including a reception, pool, sauna, fitness area, movie theater, and golf simulator. This breathtaking residence will exceed the highest expectations of luxury living.

OFFERED AT Price upon request
INQUIRIES **Svoboda & Williams**, svoboda-williams.com
ASSOCIATE Michaela Koudelová, michaela.koudelova @svoboda-williams.com, +420 257 328 281
ON THE WEB Search for C59898

PURE RELAXATION

SAINT JORIOZ, HAUTE-SAVOIE

- **Five bedrooms and three baths**
- **Breathtaking mountain and lake views**
- **Beautifully renovated interiors**

Relaxation awaits at this unique property, encompassing almost one acre (0.4 ha) on the shore of Lake Annecy, where the water shimmers between turquoise and emerald in the changing light. Exceptional views can be enjoyed from the garden, which delivers a panorama across the water, surrounding mountains, and fairytale castle at Duingt. The highest-quality materials can be found at every turn throughout the fully renovated 3,014 sq ft (280 sq m) home, with ample accommodation provided by a total of five bedrooms and three full baths. Set just steps from Lake Annecy, the residence provides easy access to a range of amenities and activities, from water and aerial sports to hiking and Michelin-starred dining. Conveniently located an hour's drive from Geneva International Airport, and within an hour of both the Aravis ski resorts and the 3 Valleys ski area, this stunning property offers a world of tranquility and natural splendor.

OFFERED AT €2,700,000
INQUIRIES **Agence Clerc Immobilier**, jc@agence-clerc.com,
+33 450 64 88 88, agence-clerc.com
ON THE WEB Search for C59864

FRANCE

ART DECO GLAMOUR
7TH ARRONDISSEMENT, PARIS

- **Seven-bedroom residence**
- **Central location with Eiffel Tower views**
- **Includes two additional studio apartments**

This is a sumptuous split-level apartment on the raised first floor and second floor of a magnificent Art Deco building, and it benefits from a landscaped garden enjoying superb views of the Eiffel Tower. The residence opens to a grand main entrance hall with a sweeping staircase leading to a spectacular reception room. This, in turn, gives access to a terrace and the beautiful garden, a spacious dining room, a library, a fully equipped kitchen with a pantry and utility room, and a bedroom suite. The upper floor showcases a generously proportioned master suite with a dressing room. A study, two further bedrooms with baths and garden vistas, a fourth bedroom, another bath, and a compact studio apartment with a shower room can also be found on this level. Also included are a garden-level studio apartment with its own kitchen and a bath, and three parking spaces. This is an exceptional dwelling in an equally exceptional location.

OFFERED AT €15,000,000
INQUIRIES **Belles Demeures de France (Daniel Féau Conseil Immobilier)**,
belles-demeures-de-france.com
ASSOCIATE Marie-Hélène Lundgreen, mhl@bdfrance.fr,
+33 6 60 34 14 62
ON THE WEB Search for C59884

SEA-VIEW VILLA
PUNTA D'ORO, PORTO-VECCHIO

• **Four bedrooms and four full baths**
• **Covered terraces, pool, and Jacuzzi**

Located in a prestigious gated community, close to the spectacular bay of Santa Giulia, this villa boasts beautiful sea views. With a desirable situation, hidden away from the outside world, the home benefits from supreme privacy and uninterrupted vistas. The property is positioned on a well-maintained 0.64-acre (0.25 ha) lot, the landscaping integrated into the environment with a Mediterranean garden enhanced by a variety of indigenous plants. Large covered terraces open towards the sea, perfect for relaxing, entertaining, and alfresco dining. A heated swimming pool and a Jacuzzi overlooking the azure ocean complete the idyllic outdoor space. Inside, four bedrooms and four full baths deliver accommodation for guests, while the spacious living room with fireplace is a wonderfully comfortable retreat. This breathtaking family residence offers a rare opportunity to join the highly sought-after community of Punta d'Oro—a magical neighborhood with easy access to the beach.

OFFERED AT €3,500,000
INQUIRIES **Corse Prestige Immobilier**, corseprestige.com
ASSOCIATE Emmanuel Castellani, infos@corseprestige.com, +33 6 12 85 05 77
ON THE WEB Search for C59896

FRANCE

CONTEMPORARY PROPERTY
CIBOURE, AQUITAINE

• **Superb master suite with ocean views**
• **Expansive heated pool**

Located on the beautiful Bordagain hillside, this unique contemporary home commands panoramic views over the spectacular Saint-Jean-de-Luz bay. Completed in 2009, the majestic residence is set in nearly 1.5 acres (0.6 ha) of lush grounds and offers almost 6,500 sq ft (604 sq m) of living space. Each of the principal rooms on the ground level enjoys stunning views of the Atlantic, and opens either on to terraces or the charming garden. Highlights include a living/reception room with fireplace, a sumptuous master suite with sitting area and ocean vistas, and a spacious gourmet kitchen equipped with the latest appliances. Upstairs are two large suites with baths, and a second wing comprises two further en suite bedrooms and a sauna. The property also boasts a self-contained studio apartment, under-floor heating, and motorized shutters, while its position means the perfectly landscaped grounds are sublimely private. This is an exquisite dwelling in a prime location.

OFFERED AT €4,950,000
INQUIRIES **Côte Ouest Immobilier**, coteouest-immobilier.com
ASSOCIATE Nicolas Descamps, ndescamps@coteouest-immobilier.fr, +33 5 59 26 82 60
ON THE WEB Search for C59707

FRANCE

ISLAND RETREAT
BADEN, MORBIHAN

- **Secluded three-bedroom villa**
- **Beautiful water views**

Just five minutes from the mainland by boat, this tranquil island retreat nestles on the edge of an extensive pine forest. The charming main villa offers unobstructed sea views from every room, and expansive living spaces lead out to a teak waterfront deck via stylish sliding doors. There are three bedrooms, one of which is en suite, a well-equipped kitchen, a main-floor bath, and an upstairs shower room. Highest quality materials, techniques, and fixtures are in evidence throughout the home, including brushed stainless steel, natural slate, parquet wood flooring, and a traditional Godin stove in the superb kitchen. An independent power generator, solar panels and storage batteries, a water desalination system, and a large water tank mean the estate is entirely autonomous. As well as a private landing deck, the acreage also encompasses three wooden outbuildings, ranging in size from 322 sq ft (30 sq m) to 538 sq ft (50 sq m), offering plenty of potential for a wide range of additional facilities.

OFFERED AT €3,150,000
INQUIRIES **David Bilder Real Estate**, davidbilder.com
ASSOCIATE David Bilder, david@davidbilder.com, +33 6 60 10 07 00
ON THE WEB Search for C59952

FRANCE

SOPHISTICATED SECLUSION
GORDES, PROVENCE-ALPES-CÔTE D'AZUR

- **Breathtaking views over the Luberon region**
- **Stunning seven-bedroom home**

This sumptuously renovated property is located at the heart of 29 acres (12 ha) with supremely peaceful landscaped gardens. Offering sublime panoramic views over the Luberon region, toward the Montagne Sainte-Victoire near Aix-en-Provence, the setting feels fabulously secluded, yet is just 15 minutes from the charming village and cultural hub of Gordes.

The south-facing main residence comprises seven bedrooms and seven baths, with interior highlights including a large kitchen, a library, and a home theater. Splendid architecture abounds, delivering bright living spaces, high-quality materials, and refined finishing touches. Every detail and modern convenience has been considered to make this a delightful retreat whatever the season. A superb pool with pool house, gorgeous exterior lounge, tennis court, guest annex, and staff quarters are additional luxuries. Immaculately private and sophisticated, and surrounded by nature, this exceptional home exceeds all expectations.

OFFERED AT €8,800,000
INQUIRIES **Michaël Zingraf Real Estate**, michaelzingraf.com
ASSOCIATE Catriona Ghione, gordes@michaelzingraf.com, +33 490 72 06 06
ON THE WEB Search for C59857

THE CASTLE
VILLENEUVE-LES-AVIGNON, GARD

- **16 bedrooms and 12 full baths**
- **Outdoor heated pool in park-like gardens**
- **Historic architectural features**

Dating back to the 16th century, when it was a coaching house in the service of the bishops of Avignon, this beautiful family castle is steeped in rich history that complements its sublime architectural grandeur. The carefully restored living space extends over some 16,146 sq ft (1,500 sq m) with breathtaking period details,

superb decorative design features, and generous volumes throughout. The sprawling interiors encompass a total of 16 bedrooms and 12 full baths, alongside a library, grand dining room, and a collection of graceful reception rooms, making the property ideal for entertaining. Like the house, the grounds deliver enviable space, spanning 5.9 acres (2.4 ha) including an exquisite park with mature trees and a rose garden, and a large heated swimming pool with pool house from which to enjoy the tranquil surroundings. A caretaker's cottage completes this incredible estate, which offers endless potential, just minutes from Avignon.

OFFERED AT €4,480,000
INQUIRIES **Poncet & Poncet**,
contact@poncet-poncet.com,
+33 4 67 02 03 31,
poncet-poncet.com
ON THE WEB Search for C59911

FRANCE

GRAND VINEYARD DOMAINE
BERGERAC, DORDOGNE

- Vineyard producing high-quality wines
- Three beautiful stone residences

This magnificent vineyard estate on 123 acres (50 ha) of predominantly south-facing slopes offers one of the finest terroirs of the Côtes de Duras. It comprises approximately 84 acres (34 ha) of mature vines, three stone residences, a state-of-the-art winery, a commercial store and tasting room, a barrel store room, and farm operating equipment. The vines themselves are between 10 and 35 years old, of multiple grape varieties: Sémillon, Sauvignon Blanc, Cabernet Sauvignon, Merlot, and Cabernet Franc, and produce around 200,000 bottles a year. The main home is a six-bedroom villa delivering panoramic views over the idyllic landscape and includes an ample terrace and a pool with pool house. There is also a cellar, guest quarters, and a manager's house with up to four bedrooms. The estate is sold as a business including all equipment, staff, goodwill, and stock. The business also has an active wine club with more than 900 members that hold non-controlling interests.

OFFERED AT €3,861,952
INQUIRIES Vineyards-Bordeaux,
vineyardsbordeaux.com
ASSOCIATE Michael Baynes,
info@vineyardsbordeaux.com,
+33 6 17 77 76 25
ON THE WEB Search for C59919

BEACHFRONT MAJESTY

PORTO HELI, ARGOLIDA

- **Seven bedrooms and eight baths**
- **30 acres with pool and sheltered beaches**
- **Just two hours' drive from Athens airport**

In the heart of cosmopolitan Porto Heli, this romantic hideaway is set on a pristine white-sand beach lapped by turquoise waters. The prestigious 30-acre (12 ha) residence delivers rolling hills, lush vegetation, and more than 3,000 ft (914 m) of coastline with two beaches and safe anchorage, providing total privacy.

The 6,835 sq ft (635 sq m) villa is defined by a relaxed aesthetic, boasting six comfortable en suite bedrooms, an inviting living room with fireplace, a home theater, playroom, and staff quarters. Two kitchens make catering a breeze, while a 30-seat outdoor dining table serves up beach and sunset panoramas in a spectacular setting for gatherings. Behind the house, a secluded swimming pool, Caribbean-style bar, and outdoor lounge area provide another unique place to entertain. This hidden jewel can be divided into 13 plots, offering the potential to build additional structures to create a one-of-a-kind estate in a prime spot.

OFFERED AT Price upon request
INQUIRIES **Ploumis Sotiropoulos Real Estate**, ploumis-sotiropoulos.gr
ASSOCIATE Christina Koutroumpa, ps@ploumis-sotiropoulos.gr, +30 210 364 3112
ON THE WEB Search for C59848

SAN ELMO LODGE
DALKEY, DUBLIN

- **Tranquil, secluded location**
- **Contemporary, light-filled interiors**
- **Three bedrooms and three full baths**

An ultimate coastal retreat of architectural significance and international standard awaits at San Elmo Lodge. This fabulous villa is set within walled grounds, high above the sea at stunning Killiney Bay. Dublin is within easy reach, yet is a world away from this dramatic landscape. Exceptionally well designed by dePaor architects, the modern property has been integrated beautifully into its intriguing split-level site. The minimalist, geometric layout is complemented by open-plan spaces, engineered timber floors, and vast glass walls framing the wonderful water views. An air of calm pervades the pared-back yet elegant residence, which is nestled in a 0.4-acre (0.16 ha) site amid well-kept gardens mostly laid to lawn surrounded by striking granite walls. Behind this, the natural woodland backdrop of mature pine trees provides shelter and serenity, with the scent of the ocean and eucalyptus trees generating a memorable sensory delight.

OFFERED AT €4,650,000
INQUIRIES **Sherry FitzGerald**, sherryfitz.ie
ASSOCIATE Rosie Mulvany, rosie.mulvany@sherryfitz.ie, +353 1 275 1000
ON THE WEB Search for C59928

BALCONE SULL'ARNO
FLORENCE

- **Walking distance to cultural monuments**
- **Elegant finishes throughout**

Situated in an enviable position in the heart of historic Florence, in a secure area near the US Embassy, this beautiful three-bedroom, four-bath luxury apartment boasts impressive living space with spectacular views of the Arno River. The interiors comprise 3,551 sq ft (330 sq m) and feature a living room with fireplace, coffered ceiling, and access to the balcony with sublime river vistas; a TV room with bar; dining room; well-equipped kitchen; and intricately frescoed anteroom. Thoughtfully restored and enriched with lavish finishes throughout, the residence displays a host of sophisticated touches, such as parquet and Carrara marble flooring, molded ceilings, trompe-l'oeil paintings, and multiple fireplaces. Ideally located for local restaurants, shops, and cultural monuments, the property is a short walk from some of the city's finest attractions, including the church of Santa Maria Novella, the Basilica di San Lorenzo, Palazzo Pitti, and the Uffizi Gallery. This is a fabulous home rich in Italian charm.

OFFERED AT €2,980,000
INQUIRIES **Agenzia Romolini**
Immobiliare Srl, romolini.com
ASSOCIATE Riccardo Romolini,
info@romolini.com,
+39 0575 788 948, +39 3356 960 513
ON THE WEB Search for C60011

ITALY

VILLA STELLA MARINA
PORTO CERVO, SARDINIA

- **Five bedrooms and six baths**
- **Direct beach access**

A masterpiece in the heart of one of the most glamorous residential areas in Costa Smeralda, this charming villa boasts a prime location alongside an exclusive lifestyle. Sitting just moments from the sea, close to the chic Hotel Cala di Volpe and picturesque Pevero Golf Club, Villa Stella Marina is surrounded by pristine gardens that provide sublime privacy and a spectacular blaze of color and perfume. The five-bedroom, six-bath enclave has two private entrances, with more than 2,900 sq ft (269 sq m) of living space across three levels. Terraces and porches with panoramic views cater for indoor–outdoor living, and luxurious verandas are suited to both quiet relaxation or large-scale entertaining. An enviable southwest aspect, gorgeous swimming pool, authentic barbecue, and direct beach access add to the residence's alfresco appeal. Characterized by the region's distinctive architectural style, and featuring traditional materials, this property is the essence of Mediterranean perfection.

OFFERED AT €7,000,000
INQUIRIES **Immobilsarda Srl**,
immobilsarda.com
ASSOCIATE Julia Bracco,
portocervo@immobilsarda.com,
+39 0789 909 000
ON THE WEB Search for C57138

THE RELAIS
ALVITO, FROSINONE

- **Surrounded by a spectacular national park**
- **Currently used as a hotel**

This charming property is nestled in the hills surrounding the Comino Valley, within the spectacular Abruzzo national park. A main residence of 3,120 sq ft (290 sq m) features a double living room that opens to an expansive terrace, and a well-equipped industrial kitchen, while a marble staircase leads up to a second living room with kitchenette and two en suite bedrooms. A split-level guest suite with its own entrance can be found on the lower level, which also boasts a 1,937 sq ft (180 sq m) space ideal for use as a wellness center. Elsewhere, the hotel accommodation comprises nine air-conditioned bedrooms, each with its own private bath and a garden or balcony. A large restaurant can cater for up to 150 people, and overlooks the pool, while incredible grounds comprise 9.9 acres (4 ha) with an orchard and a 19th-century farmhouse ripe for restoration. Equidistant from Naples, Rome, and Pescara, the estate is well connected by road, and is also equipped with a landing strip for ultra-light aircraft.

OFFERED AT Price upon request
INQUIRIES La Commerciale Srl, lacommercialerealty.it
ASSOCIATE Maurizio Pezzetta, lacommerciale@lacommerciale.org, +39 063 200 613
ON THE WEB Search for C59886

MONACO

SEAFRONT MASTERPIECE
GOLDEN SQUARE, MONTE CARLO

• **Contemporary two-bedroom apartment**
• **Central location with sublime sea views**

This stunning turnkey apartment is located on a high floor of the prestigious Mirabeau residence, famous for its perfect situation on Golden Square, facing the sea. The property has been completely renovated and decorated with the most luxurious finishes. There are Bianco Lasa marble floors in the living spaces, oak parquet floors in the two bedrooms, and a state-of-the-art home automation system throughout. Much attention has been given to the extensive living and dining area that opens on to a generous terrace with magical sea views. A sumptuous kitchen in gleaming waxed concrete anthracite has top-of-the-range appliances and a striking floor-to-ceiling glass wine cave, and blends with the living space through smoked gray glass sliding doors. The master suite boasts a walk-in closet and a stylish bath with an illuminated gray onyx back wall, and a second bedroom also features its own bath. Both offer incredible casino and port vistas, making the most of the prime location.

OFFERED AT €21,950,000
INQUIRIES Hammer Draff Great Properties, hammerdraff.com
ASSOCIATE Laurent Locchi, info@hammerdraff.com, +377 97 97 63 33
ON THE WEB Search for C59909

MOROCCO

VILLA SIDURA
AMELKIS, MARRAKECH

- **10 bedrooms and 10 full baths**
- **Close to three prestigious golf courses**

A sumptuous blend of traditional Moroccan and contemporary elements, Villa Sidura is a heavenly retreat just 10 minutes away from the vibrant and bustling city of Marrakech. The 12,916 sq ft (1,200 sq m) property features refined architecture, beautiful decorative details, and the finest materials throughout. A haven of rest and relaxation, the residence includes an array of high-end amenities such as a home theater, pool house, and plentiful living areas and intimate alcoves—ideal for indoor–outdoor entertaining. Outside, the dwelling is magnificent, boasting a traditional central courtyard, sublime glasshouse, ornate fountain, gorgeous landscaped gardens, and an enormous azure swimming pool. The stunning surroundings can be admired from the elegant covered arcade terrace with dining and living area, or the balcony that overlooks the garden. Situated on 1.7 acres (0.68 ha), this bright and comfortable family home is a Moroccan gem and a rare opportunity not to be missed.

OFFERED AT €2,400,000
INQUIRIES **Kensington Luxury Properties**, kensingtonmorocco.com
ASSOCIATE Marc Léon, marrakech@kensington.ma, +212 524 42 22 29
ON THE WEB Search for C59873

NETHERLANDS

ESTATE DEN HOOGEN GAERDE

BALKBRUG, OVERIJSSEL

- **Expansive grounds with a field of solar panels**
- **Thatched farmhouse plus additional buildings**
- **Large meadow—ideal for horse lovers**

Located alongside a meandering stream, this estate perfectly blends historical charm with modern luxury living. The extensive farmhouse dates back to 1806 and has been renovated to a high standard, with original features—such as antique tiles and a marvelous thatched roof—combining with high-tech amenities.

The generous living room has a fireplace and a delightful view of the natural swimming pond. A spacious kitchen can serve the stately dining room with ease, alongside the large wine cellar. Bursting with character, the master bedroom looks out on to the bucolic landscape of the Reestdal, and its bath features a two-person whirlpool tub and steam room. The distinctive style has been maintained in the outbuildings, including an additional home that is ideal as an office or guest accommodation. A pathway leads to the park-like garden with wonderful flowers, a vegetable garden, and a fruit orchard, every bit as enchanting as the property itself.

OFFERED AT €1,985,000
INQUIRIES **Residence 365 BV**, r365.nl
ASSOCIATE Jan Wassink, j.wassink@r365.nl, +31 65 124 2357, denhoogengaerde.nl
ON THE WEB Search for C59918

PORTUGAL

MAGNIFICENT PROPERTY
VILA DO CONDE, PORTO

- **Within easy reach of the city center**
- **Five bedrooms and eight baths**

The single-story construction of this stunning villa combines contemporary architecture with an ultra-luxurious interior. Superb materials, such as travertine marble, have been used to set a chic, modern tone, while soaring ceilings and full-height windows frame the sumptuous garden and allow interiors to be flooded with natural light. Four living and dining areas, alongside two kitchens, add to the expansive feel. Three breathtaking en suite bedrooms, complete with dressing rooms, benefit from direct access to the grounds, with the master suite enjoying views of the pool. The property is surrounded by magnificent outdoor space with a fabulous covered patio, providing total privacy and tranquility. Elsewhere, the lower floor comprises a 10-car garage, a wine cellar, and laundry room, as well as two en suite bedrooms and a living area, which would be ideal as staff accommodation. This beautiful residence is within easy reach of the city and airport, making it the perfect getaway.

OFFERED AT Price upon request
INQUIRIES LUXIMO'S, luximos.pt
ASSOCIATE Ricardo Costa,
rp@luximos.pt, +351 224 057 008
ON THE WEB Search for C59897

PORTUGAL

HILLTOP PARADISE
SILVES, ALGARVE

- **More than 13 acres with development potential**
- **Eight bedrooms and eight full baths**

Ideally located between the Algarve mountains and the coast, this luxurious villa is set on a generous 13-acre (5.26 ha) hilltop plot with panoramic mountain and ocean vistas. The main level comprises a spacious lounge with wood-burning fireplace, fully equipped kitchen, ample dining area, and an en suite bedroom. Upstairs, there are three en suite bedrooms with hydromassage tubs and sizeable terraces that offer spectacular views, while a further bedroom suite can be found on the basement level, along with a sauna and a wine cellar. Outside, the superb landscaped gardens feature a pool with Jacuzzi, and there is also a charming three-bedroom guest cottage; orange, olive, carob, and almond trees; and a four-car garage, plus additional parking. A motion-sensor alarm, electric gated entrance, air conditioning, and under-floor heating add extra convenience to this fabulous residence, just 20 minutes from Silves, 15 minutes from Albufeira, and 30 minutes from Faro International Airport.

OFFERED AT €2,090,000
INQUIRIES **LUXIMO'S**,
vilamoura@luximos.pt,
+351 289 035 465, luximos.pt
ON THE WEB Search for C59867

SEA-VIEW SPLENDOR
OEIRAS, LISBON

• **Close to local amenities**
• **Bright, open interiors**

A prime location and spectacular sea views are just two of the myriad selling points of this beautiful six-bedroom villa. Interior space of 9,850 sq ft (915 sq m) is arranged over two main floors, plus a basement, and is filled with natural light, making the most of the tranquil vistas. The first floor takes in a pair of living rooms and a spacious dining room, overlooking the ocean and with access to a generous terrace and the sparkling pool. A superbly equipped kitchen, laundry room, bedroom suite, and a separate bath complete the level. The master suite resides on the second floor, along with another bedroom suite, and three further bedrooms—all with their own balconies and stunning seascapes. The pool is perfect for both relaxation and exercise, with an electric treadmill and plenty of room to lounge. This incredible home is located just two minutes' walk from the railway station, 10 minutes from the beach, and 15 minutes by car from the center of Lisbon and the town of Cascais.

OFFERED AT €3,300,000
INQUIRIES **Porta da Frente, Lda**, portadafrente.com
ASSOCIATE Rafael Ascenso, info@portadafrente.pt, +351 214 688 891
ON THE WEB Search for C59850

SOUTH AFRICA

MAJESTIC MOUNTAIN ESTATE
HOUT BAY, WESTERN CAPE

- Five bedrooms and four baths
- Infinity-edge pool with incredible views

Perched on Table Mountain's Twelfth Apostle, just minutes away from Llandudno Beach, the Ruyteplaats Private Mountain Estate offers an exclusive enclave from which to experience the location's lush landscape, along with a range of amenities such as tennis courts and a children's park right on the doorstep. This elegant five-bedroom residence delivers bespoke finishes throughout and is offered fully furnished. Sumptuous interiors are characterized by floor-to-ceiling sliding doors that allow uninterrupted views of the horizon. The home flows effortlessly from the vast living area to the lavish entertainment patio, where the heated infinity-edge pool seems to cascade down to the bay below. Highlights include a stunning master suite with access to the patio, and a designer kitchen featuring Caesarstone countertops. Presented in pristine condition and with top-of-the-range security, this impressive property provides the perfect blend of luxury and inspirational beauty.

OFFERED AT ZAR 28,000,000
INQUIRIES **Greeff Properties**, greeff.co.za
ASSOCIATE Lindsay Goodman, lindsay@greeff.co.za, +27 82 638 1758
ON THE WEB Search for C59950

LA ZAGALETA VILLA
BENAHAVIS, MALAGA

- **Stylish nine-bedroom home**
- **Serene woodland setting close to Marbella**

This incredible home boasts a prime location within the La Zagaleta resort, a natural forest estate of secluded valleys, wooded hills, and beauty spots extending between the mountain and sea, just 15 minutes from Marbella. The highest quality materials have been utilized throughout this enormous nine-bedroom villa. Luxuriously spacious, it features gleaming marble floors, luscious greenery, indoor and outdoor pools, and phenomenal vistas. The first floor has multiple living areas, two kitchens, and a dining room, plus two en suite bedrooms and an expansive terrace. Upstairs, the master suite and two further bedrooms, all with their own baths and terraces, can be found, as well as an office. A real highlight of the multi-use basement is its vast relaxation area, with a sauna, Turkish bath, gym, bar, and pool, as well as parking space for eight cars and storage. All levels of the house offer magnificent views of the Mediterranean Sea and the resort's two 18-hole golf courses.

OFFERED AT €14,500,000
INQUIRIES Costa Del Sol 365, costadelsol365.es
ASSOCIATE Hans Veenhuijsen, h.veenhuijsen@costadelsol365.es, +34 951 122 313
ON THE WEB Search for C59954

SPAIN

VILLA GLADIS
IBIZA

- **Pristine modern architecture**
- **11 bedrooms and 12 baths in total**
- **Swimming pool with superb ocean views**

Within an exclusive gated community, this exquisitely crafted villa has a hypnotic beauty matched only by its incomparable sea views. Crisp white walls envelop more than 9,600 sq ft (892 sq m) of living space, in which the finest quality materials and finishes take center stage. The fully equipped kitchen with high-end appliances is a chef's dream; seven bedrooms each boast an en suite bath and dressing room; and large-format picture windows frame mesmerizing vistas throughout. Outside, more than an acre (0.5 ha) of grounds encompass a spectacular terrace with outdoor dining area, a guesthouse, relaxing retreats for enjoying the long summer days, and a dazzling pool that seems to merge with sea and sky. Occupying one of the most privileged enclaves in the community, with direct access to a cove, Villa Gladis offers a magical environment that is just a short drive from the center of Ibiza Town and only 20 minutes from the international airport.

OFFERED AT Price upon request
INQUIRIES Estela Exclusive Homes, estelaexclusivehomes.com
ASSOCIATE Sandra Tejero, request@estelaexclusivehomes.com, +34 971 931 562
ON THE WEB Search for C585540

CONTEMPORARY GEM

LA CORONA, JÁVEA

- **Four bedrooms and five full baths**
- **Panoramic coastal views**
- **Fabulous outdoor space with pool**

Located in a prestigious residential area, this 3,778 sq ft (351 sq m) villa is a fusion of modern elegance and original design. Natural light floods the ample spaces throughout the four floors, which include a dining room, gourmet kitchen with laundry area, and pantry. Among the four generous bedrooms is a master suite with dressing room. Elsewhere, a library/office area, multipurpose room, garage for two cars, and carport for four additional vehicles add convenient extras. The home is equipped for all seasons, with awnings, large windows, air conditioning, under-floor heating, and electric blinds, creating the perfect ambience morning, noon, and night. Outside, a number of terraced areas offer magnificent places from which to enjoy the panoramic vistas, as well as a superb pool, while a striking garden boasts verdant Mediterranean flora. This residence is ideally set close to the port of Jávea, the nearby yacht club, and the area's most beautiful beaches.

OFFERED AT €1,550,000
INQUIRIES **Rimontgó**, rimontgo.com
ASSOCIATE Antonio Ribes,
rimontgo@rimontgo.es,
+34 965 791 035
ON THE WEB Search for C59860

SWEDEN

SEAFRONT GLAMOUR
TÄBY, STOCKHOLM

- Dock with space for several boats
- Immaculate main villa plus guesthouses
- Bright, airy contemporary design

This brand new, luxury waterfront property offers sheer perfection throughout, with the highest standard of finishes and the finest handpicked materials from around the world. Inside the main six-bedroom, four-bath villa, which spans nearly 9,000 sq ft (836 sq m) of chic living space, there are fabulous areas for entertaining, indoor and outdoor kitchens, a wine cellar, and a gym, while multiple fireplaces and an elevator between floors add additional luxury and convenience. A separate guest apartment in the primary building is joined by two standalone houses with their own living quarters plus kitchenette and sauna—providing plenty of space to host family and friends. The idyllic estate is completed by a dock with room to moor several boats, a three-car garage, and a spectacular pool. Boasting impressive water views and fantastic indoor–outdoor living, this is a unique and highly desirable offering just 20 minutes away from the heart of Stockholm.

OFFERED AT Price upon request
INQUIRIES Residence Fastighetsmäkleri, residence.se
ASSOCIATE Jonas Häggbom, jonas.haggbom@residence.se, +46 706 179 619
ON THE WEB Search for C59980

CHARACTERFUL ABODE

PRANGINS, VAUD

- **Charming period property with five bedrooms**
- **Secluded parkland setting**
- **Option to extend the original home**

Brimming with character, this beautiful home is nestled amid lush parkland, surrounded by an array of plant species that flower throughout the seasons to create a year-round sanctuary. The whole property offers an exceptional lifestyle in the heart of the charming village of Prangins. Built in 1907, the house has been renovated throughout, retaining its traditional materials to ensure the charm of yesteryear marries perfectly with today's requirements for modern comfort. On the first floor are the reception and living areas, and a magnificent veranda that opens to the grounds beyond. A marvelous second-floor master suite comprises a bedroom, a lounge or office, and a sheltered terrace, while there are three more bedrooms, a bath, and a reading corner in the attic. The fully heated basement features a wine cellar, music room, leisure area, and laundry room, plus the estate has building authorization for potential further development in the future.

OFFERED AT CHF 5,100,000
INQUIRIES SPG Finest Properties, nyon@spgfinestproperties.ch, +41 58 810 36 50, spgfinestproperties.ch
ON THE WEB Search for C59904

SWITZERLAND

VILLA CIGNO
MINUSIO, TICINO

- **Private beach and dock**
- **Six bedrooms and seven full baths**

Renovated to an incredibly high standard, this 1960 waterfront villa offers luxury living just steps from the lake. The majestic main entrance of the 8,600 sq ft (800 sq m) property leads to the grand entry foyer, with red Verona marble, mosaics, and a fountain. Elevated by the brand-new Miro & Paolo furniture, the stylish living and dining room has a custom-built bar, with a large refrigerator, and climate-controlled wine storage with room for 300 bottles. Extremely well equipped, the residence has a stunning Carlo Rampazzi-designed gourmet kitchen, plus three additional full kitchens for guests and staff. The master suite, which was recently expanded and redesigned, encompasses a remote-controlled fireplace, and a bath with hand-painted Italian ceramics and tiles. Outside, a lush south-facing garden is filled with evergreen plantings, while a barbecue and lounging areas are situated under the shade of the portico. This is a home as breathtaking as the surrounding lake and mountain views.

OFFERED AT CHF 9,900,000
INQUIRIES **Wetag Consulting Immobiliare SA**, wetag.ch
ASSOCIATE Ueli Schnorf, u.schnorf@wetag.ch, +41 91 601 04 40
ON THE WEB Search for C59905

GOLD COAST RESIDENCE
HERRLIBERG, ZURICH

- Rare opportunity in a prestigious area
- Exclusive villa with up to five bedrooms
- Indoor–outdoor living and entertaining spaces

This prestigious property, constructed in 1954, is situated in a sought-after area of Lake Zurich. Recently renovated, the impeccably designed interiors offer classic country-house style with a modern twist, while leaving plenty of scope for personalization. Spanning almost 4,300 sq ft (400 sq m), the home has four bedrooms—with the potential for five if desired—and three full baths. Highlights include a beautifully equipped kitchen and fabulous indoor–outdoor spaces that are ideal for entertaining. Bright living and dining rooms open out to idyllic terraces and seating areas within the tranquil, supremely private gardens, which deliver a unique piece of heaven overlooking the lake. With the vibrant city of Zurich just a short drive away, and the scenic surroundings of the wooded mountain of Pfannenstiel providing an array of jogging, cycling, and hiking options, this is an exquisite dwelling offering an unparalleled lakeside lifestyle.

OFFERED AT Price upon request
INQUIRIES **Wüst und Wüst AG**, wuw.ch
ASSOCIATE Annelies Wüst, annelies.wuest@wuw.ch, +41 44 388 58 38
ON THE WEB Search for C59254

UPSCALE CITY STYLE
NOTTING HILL, LONDON

- **Fabulously appointed open-plan living space**
- **Gorgeous statement pool**

Ideally located in one of the city's most desirable neighborhoods, this contemporary home is a masterpiece of design. Completely redeveloped, the house offers world-class luxury throughout, finished with immaculate up-to-the-minute interior styling that celebrates the spacious, light-filled design. The open-plan layout links a reception room, dining room, and fabulously appointed kitchen to create one superlative living space that is perfect for entertaining. Four bedrooms feature a sumptuous master suite with dressing area, while elsewhere the home benefits from dual media rooms, a gym or games room, and a dazzling indoor pool. Further highlights include a self-contained apartment with kitchen, a generous south-facing garden, and sought-after off-street parking. Complemented by its proximity to the green space of Kensington Gardens and the numerous boutiques, cafes, and restaurants of Notting Hill, this incredible urban escape is a rare and stylish package.

OFFERED AT £20,000,000
INQUIRIES **Strutt & Parker**, struttandparker.com
ASSOCIATE Miles Meacock, miles.meacock@struttandparker.com, +44 20 7221 1111
ON THE WEB Search for C59993

THE OLD RECTORY
GLOUCESTERSHIRE, ENGLAND

- Impressive pastoral residence
- Beautiful, well-maintained grounds
- Potential for development

Occupying a prime location, surrounded by breathtaking Cotswolds countryside, this incredible property displays historical charm and traditional elegance in abundance. A short drive from the market town of Cirencester, and within easy reach of Cheltenham, Oxford, and London, The Old Rectory offers country living that is as convenient as it is tranquil. Nestled amid 22 acres (8.9 ha) of pristinely maintained grounds, the estate comprises an 8,224 sq ft (764 sq m) primary house, a barn that could potentially be converted into a four-bedroom home, and a three-car garage with apartment above. The sumptuous main residence boasts six reception rooms, ideal for entertaining, plus a top-floor playroom with kitchen, a utility room, and cellar, as well as eight bedrooms and five baths. There is also a grazing license in place on the grounds for sheep, enhancing the appeal of this quintessential rural lifestyle combined with enviable levels of luxury.

OFFERED AT £5,500,000
INQUIRIES Strutt & Parker, struttandparker.com
ASSOCIATE Luke Morgan, luke.morgan@struttandparker.com, +44 20 7318 5095
ON THE WEB Search for C59995

THE LOWER COURT ESTATE
OXFORDSHIRE, ENGLAND

- **Grand Grade II* listed manor house**
- **Spectacular location among arable farmland**

The Lower Court Estate sits on the north side of the Evenlode Valley, surrounded by beautiful rolling countryside. At the heart of the property, the stunning Grade II* listed manor occupies a glorious elevated position overlooking the majesty of the surrounding valley. Behind the house lies a traditional range of Cotswold stone farm buildings and five cottages that form part

of this exceptional offering. To the west lies a charming farmstead, positioned at the foot of a long, private driveway. It comprises a range of farm buildings and a pair of semi-detached cottages, which present a fantastic opportunity for conversion into a spectacular residential property—subject to the necessary planning consent. The estate is surrounded by approximately 515 acres (208 ha) of verdant arable land. This sensational acreage is available to purchase as a whole or can be divided into carefully curated lots, offering a range of opportunities to buy into this magnificent pastoral scene close to Chipping Norton.

OFFERED AT £20,000,000
INQUIRIES **Strutt & Parker**, struttandparker.com
ASSOCIATE Mark McAndrew, mark.mcandrew @struttandparker.com, +44 20 7318 5171
ON THE WEB Search for C59996

PAIT AND WEST MONAR ESTATE
ROSS-SHIRE, SCOTLAND

- **Victorian lodge and sporting estate**
- **Spectacular Highland setting on Loch Monar**

Extending across almost 15,000 acres (6,070 ha), Pait and West Monar is a traditional Highland sporting estate providing an exceptional blend of first-class red deer stalking, grouse shooting, and trout and pike fishing among some of the most dramatic terrain anywhere in Scotland. An impeccably private escape, accessible by boat via Loch Monar and a seasonal single-track road, this extensive property offers a perfect combination of relaxation and adventure. A stalker's cottage, where the housekeeper currently resides, and a range of outbuildings are included with the acreage, along with the main residence—an impressive eight-bedroom Victorian lodge that has been thoughtfully preserved since its construction in the late 19th century. Split by a tongue of land that stretches from the top of the loch, the surroundings are divided into two "deer forests" of a similar size, providing stalking and walked-up shooting of phenomenal quality. This secluded retreat represents a once-in-a-lifetime opportunity.

OFFERED AT £2,000,000
INQUIRIES Strutt & Parker,
struttandparker.com
ASSOCIATE Robert McCulloch,
robert.mcculloch
@struttandparker.com,
+44 131 718 4593
ON THE WEB Search for C59997

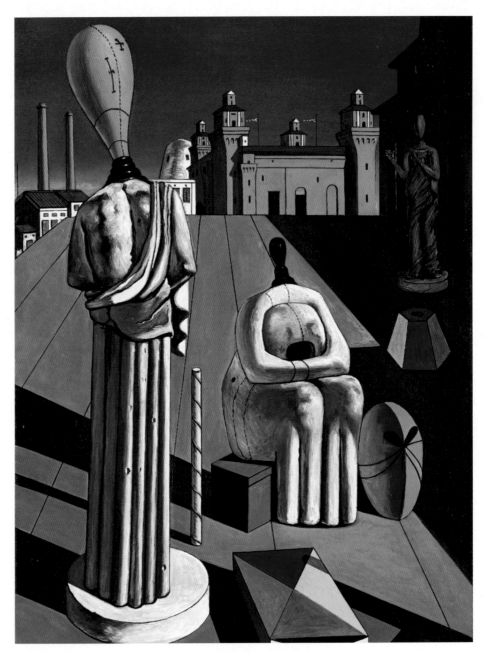

GIORGIO DE CHIRICO (1888-1978)
Le muse inquietanti
oil on canvas
38⅛ x 25⅞ in. (97 x 66 cm.)
Painted in 1962

THINKING ITALIAN
London, 4 October 2019

VIEWING
25 September-4 October
8 King Street
London SW1Y 6QT

CONTACT
Mariolina Bassetti
mbassetti@christies.com
+39 06 686 3330

CHRISTIE'S

ASIA
PACIFIC

Pages 127-137

FIJI

TROPICAL PARADISE
DENARAU ISLAND

- **Six bedrooms and eight baths**
- **Marina berth for an 80 ft (24 m) boat**

This island retreat has been custom built with a pavilion-style layout designed to maximize its unobstructed views across the South Pacific. Vaulted ceilings enhance the living space, with floor-to-ceiling glass doors bringing the outdoors in. Artisanal details feature throughout, including handcrafted wood finishes, beautiful sandstone-clad walls,

and a striking entrance foyer with sculptural skylight and internal garden. The main living pavilion is anchored by a chef's kitchen with island and scullery, while a separate media room and study add further recreation space. Lush landscaped gardens comprise oceanfront decks, a skate ramp, a firepit, a solar-heated pool, and a boat ramp for a 30 ft (9 m) vessel or seaplane. High-end resorts with fine dining and sporting facilities are a few minutes' walk away, and Nadi International Airport is less than six miles (9.6 km) from the property. A personal chef, a housekeeper, and gardeners are also available at this oceanfront slice of paradise.

OFFERED AT US$11,000,000
INQUIRIES Ken Jacobs,
kenjacobs.com.au
ASSOCIATE Ken Jacobs,
ken@kenjacobs.com.au,
+61 407 190 152,
27thepeninsula.cve.io
ON THE WEB Search for C59858

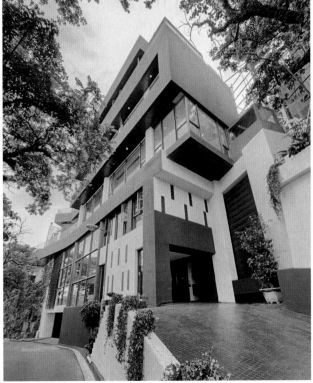

THE HIGH LIFE
POLLOCK'S PATH, THE PEAK

- **Statement home in an elevated position**
- **Four bedrooms and four full baths**
- **Panoramic views inside and out**

In a prestigious location high on The Peak, this ultramodern home offers fabulous views over Victoria Harbour and the city skyline. The highlight of the 3,649 sq ft (339 sq m) interior is the double-height great room with separated living and dining areas and floor-to-ceiling windows. All four of the bedroom suites have full baths, while the master suite also features wraparound windows, for appreciation of the setting. Outside, the potential for grand entertaining continues on a sprawling terrace with covered swing seats and a panoramic outlook. A secluded swimming pool also boasts spectacular vistas across the harbor, reaching all the way to the central business district. The CBD itself is just 20 minutes away, while elite schools, high-end shops, gourmet dining, and more can be found even closer to home. Yet, for all its access to world-class services and amenities, the property feels sublimely removed from the bustle of the city.

OFFERED AT HK$886,000,000
INQUIRIES **Landscope Christie's International Real Estate**, landscope.com
ASSOCIATE Louis Wong, louis.wong@landscope.com, +852 9871 6828
ON THE WEB Search for C59856

DETAIL OF AN ILLUSTRATED BIFOLIUM FROM THE *NAHJ AL-FARADIS* 'PATHWAY TO THE HEAVENS'
Commissioned by Sultan Abu Sa'id, Timurid Herat, circa 1465
Opaque pigments and gold on paper
folio 16 ¼ x 11 ⅞in. (41.4 x 30.3cm.)
£700,000–1,000,000

**ART OF THE ISLAMIC AND INDIAN
WORLDS INCLUDING ORIENTAL
RUGS AND CARPETS**

London, 24 October 2019

VIEWING
19-23 October
8 King Street
London SW1Y 6QT

CONTACT
Behnaz Atighi Moghaddam
batighi@christies.com
+44 (0)207 389 2509

CHRISTIE'S

MALDIVES

AMILLARAH PRIVATE ISLANDS
NEAR MALÉ, NORTH MALÉ ATOLL

• Unique tailor-made private islands
• The ultimate hideaway

The dream of owning a private island can now be made reality—thanks to Amillarah. An incredible lagoon has been divided into a limited number of water plots, each with its own private island residence just 10 minutes by boat from the international airport, where private airplanes can easily and safely be parked. Combining this amazing location with the craftsmanship of the Dutch leads to the first man-made, self-sufficient, and eco-friendly private islands, which can be fully customized in terms of size, shape, and style to exactly reflect individual lifestyles and demands. The islands are developed with the latest state-of-the-art green technology, which keeps their environmental impact to a minimum. Each one promises to be the ultimate hideaway, or the base for holidays with friends and family. Activities range from swimming, diving, and snorkeling, to simply soaking up the sun, listening to the gentle waves, and enjoying a cocktail before dinner.

OFFERED AT Price upon request
INQUIRIES **Dutch Docklands Maldives**,
dutchdocklands-maldives.com,
amillarah.com
ASSOCIATE Jasper Mulder,
jaspermulder@amillarah.com,
+960 333 6664

UNRIVALED ARTISTRY

ROCKCLIFFE PARK, OTTAWA

- **Sought-after Old Village location**
- **Designed to bring the outdoors in**

Setting a new high standard of elegance and sophistication, this timeless residence is located on a quiet street in a prime location. Sitting high on a rare, south-facing lot, the home's stone exterior is breathtaking while the interiors are flooded with natural light. With a layout that unfolds beautifully into open-plan living spaces, entertaining is a dream. Richly detailed ceilings, exquisite moldings, and a stunning fireplace adorn the great room. The sumptuous dining room enjoys southern exposure and opens to a covered terrace with views of the tranquil infinity-edge pool, hot tub, and meticulously landscaped gardens. Further highlights include a custom chef's kitchen that is characterized by hand-glazed cabinetry, and a phenomenal main floor master suite with a fabulous walk-in closet and an en suite bath with glass shower and separate soaking tub. This well-designed and impeccably finished property is one of Rockcliffe Park's most prestigious homes.

OFFERED AT C$5,745,000
INQUIRIES Marilyn Wilson Dream Properties Inc. Brokerage, dreamproperties.com
ASSOCIATES Marilyn Wilson, marilyn@dreamproperties.com, +1 613 842 5000, Reba Wilson, reba@dreamproperties.com, +1 613 842 5000
ON THE WEB Search for C59407

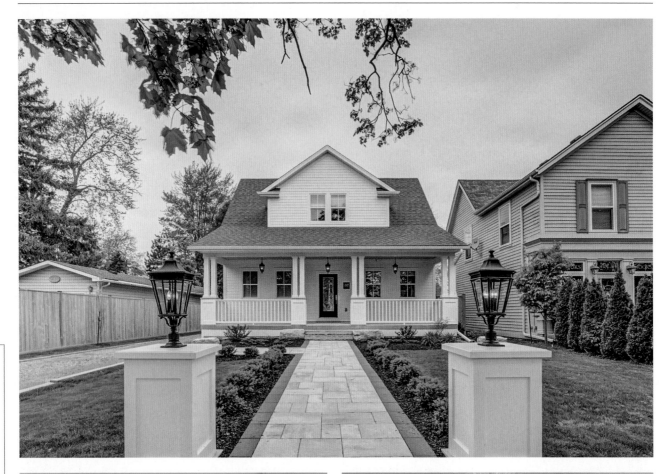

CLASSIC LUXURY
NIAGARA-ON-THE-LAKE

- **Five bedrooms and five-and-a-half baths**
- **Stylish, light-filled interiors**

Recently renovated, this stunning custom-built home offers immaculate finishes throughout 4,200 sq ft (390 sq m) of generous living space, introduced by a striking front porch. Designed around a luxurious open-plan layout, neutral decor allows the soaring ceilings, oversized windows, and handsome wood flooring to shine. Spacious principal rooms include a gourmet kitchen with quartz countertops and a center island. This opens to a bright dining area as well as to the gracious living room with fireplace and French doors to a superb covered porch. A master suite with spa-like bath and walk-in closet is also incorporated into the main floor, while three additional bedrooms can be found on the upper level. The lower floor is fully furnished to include a recreation room with beautiful bar area, exercise space, and a fifth bedroom. Further accommodation is provided in the fully equipped coach house. Combining elegance and comfort, this is a modern family residence beyond compare.

OFFERED AT C$2,498,000
INQUIRIES **Niagara-on-the-Lake Realty, Ltd**, notlrealty.com
ASSOCIATE Thomas Elltoft, tom@notlrealty.com, +1 905 380 8012
ON THE WEB Search for C59869

ELEGANT STYLE
LITTLE BURGUNDY, MONTREAL

- **Sought-after central location**
- **Two-unit custom-built retail space below**

Grand 18th-century carved entrance doors and antique salvaged bricks set an opulent tone for this sophisticated two-story residence. Soaring ceilings, detailed crown moldings, wide-plank hemlock and cherry flooring, and beautiful ceiling corbels enhance the old-world ambience —while the modern construction masterfully incorporates high-tech additions such as thermal sound-proofed windows and a superb integrated sound system. The primary floor encompasses large living and dining areas, as well as a cozy den and dream kitchen where a stunning 10 ft (3 m) granite island is joined by poplar cabinetry. A wet bar and six-burner gas stove complete the luxurious finish. Upstairs, four bedrooms delight with 19th-century pine-paneled doors salvaged from a convent, and the master suite includes a balcony and lavish bath. A magical 3,000 sq ft (279 sq m) roof garden with a cedar deck and barbecue area showcases mature cedar and hydrangea trees, and completes this impressive dwelling.

OFFERED AT C$4,245,000
INQUIRIES **Profusion Realty Inc.**, profusion.global
ASSOCIATE Christina Miller, christina@christinamiller.ca, +1 514 934 2480
ON THE WEB Search for C59932

WATERFRONT GRANDEUR
IVRY-SUR-LE-LAC, LAURENTIDES

- **Stunning lake and mountain views**
- **Extensive living and entertaining spaces**
- **Additional two-bedroom guesthouse**

In the heart of a highly desirable community, this impressive home combines outstanding craftsmanship, intricate detailing, and richly appointed rooms throughout. Open-plan living spaces blend stone and wood to create timeless rustic charm. The generous living room, with a double-height cathedral ceiling and multilevel stone fireplace, is flooded with natural light from stunning floor-to-ceiling windows. This, alongside a gourmet kitchen and formal dining room, sets the stage for entertaining. On the second floor, a bright balcony gives way to two charming bedrooms, with the expansive master suite enjoying private access to a terrace with panoramic views. A two-level guesthouse, adjacent to the garage, has a beautiful kitchen that opens to a dining room, and a mezzanine level that can provide further accommodation. Outside, the covered porch offers entertaining space, while picturesque paths lead to the lake where two boat slips and a new dock await.

OFFERED AT C$2,100,000
INQUIRIES **Profusion Realty Inc.**, profusion.global
ASSOCIATE Christina Miller, christina@christinamiller.ca, +1 514 934 2480
ON THE WEB Search for C59933

QUEBEC, CANADA

CASA BOKKE
FUNDADORES, SAN JOSÉ DEL CABO

- **Five bedrooms and five full baths**
- **Golf course just steps away**
- **Bright, contemporary, open-plan living**

Located in the exclusive golf community of Fundadores, this fantastic two-story home delivers spectacular views of both the ocean and golf course. Ideal as either a full-time home or a luxury vacation retreat, Casa Bokke offers 8,848 sq ft (822 sq m) of beautiful living space, with extensive storage throughout.

The incredible interiors are characterized by vaulted ceilings with exposed beams, plantation shutters, and an expansive open-plan living area. Five bedrooms and five-and-a-half baths provide plenty of accommodation for family and guests, while an updated garage has room for two vehicles or space for boats, Jet Skis, or other watercraft. A modernized chef's kitchen boasts state-of-the-art appliances and a large island, ideal for entertaining. Outside, there is a voluminous living area with a breathtaking infinity-edge pool and spa, overlooking a lush garden that backs on to the fairway, as well as the ocean beyond.

OFFERED AT US$2,200,000
INQUIRIES 2Seas Los Cabos,
2seasloscabos.com
ASSOCIATE Ramiro Palenque Bullrich, ramiro@2seasloscabos.com, +521 624 118 1387
ON THE WEB Search for C59782

BEACHFRONT PARADISE
DIAMANTE, CABO SAN LUCAS

- **Stylish three-bedroom apartment**
- **Prime location in a first-class luxury resort**

The Ocean Club Residences (OCR) is a new luxury development, which offers enviable living, with impressive facilities, directly on the beach. This three-bedroom, three-bath condominium is the first multi-unit beachfront home available. It is steps away from the Pacific Ocean, and boasts breathtaking sunset views from the private patio. The OCR will feature

a host of amenities, including expansive pools with swim-up bars, restaurants, a fitness center, spa, kids' club, shops, and luxurious lounge areas. The cornerstone of the OCR project will be Diamante's signature first-class service, and access to two world-class golf courses, designed by Tiger Woods and Davis Love III—the latter of which is currently ranked 36th of all golf courses in the world. Residents will have access to the 10-acre (4 ha) crystal lagoon, six miles (9.65 km) of hiking trails, and a pristine sandy beach stretching almost 1.5 miles (2.4 km) from the edge of the pool, completing this outstanding opportunity.

OFFERED AT US$1,400,000
INQUIRIES 2Seas Los Cabos,
2seasloscabos.com
ASSOCIATE Ramiro Palenque Bullrich, ramiro@2seasloscabos.com, +521 624 118 1387
ON THE WEB Search for C59977

CASA ZÓCALO
CENTRO, SAN MIGUEL DE ALLENDE

- **Gorgeous grounds with heated pool**
- **Eight fireplaces, both indoor and out**

Hidden away behind abundant vegetation at the end of a private street, Casa Zócalo offers the epitome of luxury indoor–outdoor living, with wonderful views of the countryside and historic San Miguel. Steps lead past a beautiful heated pool, complete with dramatic waterfall, to the first level where an outdoor living room boasts panoramas over the lush, landscaped gardens.

Another short staircase introduces the primary interior living area, rich with traditional detail characterized by stenciled and beamed ceilings. A dining room and family room are joined by a superb gourmet kitchen with new cabinetry, countertops, and appliances. Six bedrooms include two guest rooms, each with a terrace overlooking the pool, and two master suites that have terraces of their own. Eight outdoor seating areas and a poolside casita with full kitchen provide an array of spaces from which to soak up the serenity of the lavish gardens or enjoy alfresco dining. A garage and home security system complete the sublime picture.

OFFERED AT US$2,495,000
INQUIRIES **CDR San Miguel**, cdrsanmiguel.com
ASSOCIATES Jessica Patterson, jessica@cdrsanmiguel.com, +52 1 415 105 6572, Peggy Taylor, peggy@cdrsanmiguel.com +52 1 415 101 0058
ON THE WEB Search for C59880

VILLA DEL PARQUE
PARQUE JUAREZ, SAN MIGUEL DE ALLENDE

- **Three-bedroom home with roof terrace**
- **Indoor and outdoor entertaining spaces**

Encircled by lush, tropical gardens, stunning Villa del Parque boasts an incredible location. The splendid natural surroundings are further enhanced by the proximity of magnificent Parque Juarez, reached through a charming garden door built into a wall that borders the property. Inside, an airy, open-plan layout is anchored by a sumptuous living and dining

area with a large fireplace and French doors that open on to the terrace and gardens. The single-level living space also features an eat-in kitchen, and a total of three bedrooms includes a dazzling master suite. Residents and guests can retreat to the spacious rooftop terrace for serene sunsets surrounded by treetops and glimpses of towering churches, or the ground-level covered terrace to take in vistas of the verdant gardens from the relaxed bar area with carved cantera stone fireplace. Sited just a short walk from the historic center of San Miguel, Villa del Parque is a spectacular, secure offering, rich with natural beauty.

OFFERED AT US$1,200,000
INQUIRIES **CDR San Miguel**, cdrsanmiguel.com
ASSOCIATE Anne Jones, annejones@cdrsanmiguel.com, +52 1 415 153 3770
ON THE WEB Search for C59879

GUANAJUATO, MEXICO

MEXICO CITY, MEXICO

EXCLUSIVE CITY RETREAT
CLUB DE GOLF SANTA FE

- **Three bedrooms and five full baths**
- **Bright, spacious interiors**
- **Spectacular views**

Within one of the country's premier business districts lies an urban oasis that represents one of the rare green spaces left in Mexico City —Bosques de Santa Fe. Inside this exclusive community, which includes a nine-hole golf course and a 61.5-acre (25 ha) forest among a range of other world-class facilities, stands this magnificent home. A perfect blend of modern and classical design, the house harmoniously integrates into the surrounding woods through its infinity-edge garden, giving owners a sense of peaceful seclusion. Conceived by renowned Mexican architect Enrique Bardasano, the remarkable residence is arranged around a beautiful inner courtyard filled with natural light, which—combined with the dwelling's double-height ceilings and towering glass doors to the garden—provides a feeling of space and grandeur. Brimming with luxury finishes, this tranquil property offers a retreat from city life, yet is still close to all major amenities.

OFFERED AT US$6,850,000
INQUIRIES LUX Bienes Raices,
luxmx.com
ASSOCIATE Joseph Lown,
joseph@luxmx.com,
+521 415 103 3374
ON THE WEB Search for C59889

REFINED ELEGANCE

SAN PATRICIO, SAN PEDRO GARZA GARCÍA

- **Stunning grounds with pool and terrace**
- **Four bedrooms and six baths**

Positioned within one of the most exclusive and sought-after residential communities in the area, the setting of this charming custom-built dwelling is just as grand as its exceptional interior offerings. Designed with elegant living and entertaining in mind, the spacious home blends contemporary style with sophisticated refinement to deliver a perfectly curated space.

Beautifully crafted with the utmost attention to detail, immaculate finishes can be found throughout the residence, which provides four bedrooms and six full baths, an impressive gourmet kitchen, a family room, a home theater, and a games room. Stunning high ceilings and abundant natural light are a theme throughout the space, particularly in the gorgeous living room where fabulous floor-to-ceiling windows frame sublime views. Moving outside, relaxing gardens feature a spectacular swimming pool and the ultimate entertaining terrace with outdoor kitchen. An elevator, gym, and smart-home system complete this masterful property.

OFFERED AT MXN 85,000,000
INQUIRIES **Gerencia RED Grupo Inmobiliario**, gerenciared.com
ASSOCIATE Gerardo M Gutierrez, gmgutierrez@gerenciared.com, +1 818 363 1212
ON THE WEB Search for C59913

ARIZONA, UNITED STATES

TIMELESS PRESTIGE
PARADISE VALLEY, MARICOPA COUNTY

- **Five bedrooms and nine full baths**
- **Mountain and golf course views**

In a privileged position atop a hillside lot, this timeless residence looks out across the Paradise Valley Country Club golf course to the mountains by day and the sparkling city lights at night. Classic elegance and quality workmanship define the property, which was built in 1993 to a design by the renowned architect George Christensen. Highlights of the 10,500 sq ft (975 sq m) floor plan include a pitched, beamed ceiling in the spacious living room, wood and stone flooring, cantera stone details, custom ironwork, and a wine room. The charming kitchen has a butler's pantry and opens to the family room, while glass doors on the entertainment level lead to a stunning patio, swimming pool, and barbecue. A total of five bedrooms and nine full baths takes in a lavish master suite with a wood-paneled office, dual baths, and two closets. Gorgeous grounds are gated with a scenic driveway that leads to ample parking, adding to the potential for large-scale entertaining at this fantastic family home.

OFFERED AT US$4,250,000
INQUIRIES Walt Danley Realty,
waltdanley.com
ASSOCIATE Walt Danley,
walt@waltdanley.com,
+1 480 991 2050
ON THE WEB Search for C59988

CALIFORNIA, UNITED STATES

PRIME LOCATION
PASADENA, LOS ANGELES COUNTY

- **Newly constructed three-bedroom townhouse**
- **Timeless architecture and luxurious amenities**

Recently constructed as part of the third phase of development in Pasadena's highly sought-after Town & Country community, this three-bedroom, three-bath Italian Renaissance-style townhouse is a prime offering. The home's interiors are filled with light thanks to broad windows and French doors looking out on to shaded courtyards. Period details are softly accented by recessed lighting, and upscale features include porcelain tile floors, Berber wall-to-wall carpeting, and wide-plank wooden floors. Multizone air-conditioning and large double-paned aluminum windows assure comfort throughout. Superb baths boast quartz countertops and imported European faucets, while a custom kitchen features stainless-steel appliances and modern cabinets. In the heart of Pasadena, the property is close to The Shops on Lake Avenue, The Huntington Library with its art collections and botanical gardens, top schools, and the shops and restaurants of Old Town, delivering a wide range of leisure options.

OFFERED AT US$1,155,000
INQUIRIES Dilbeck Estates,
dilbeck.com
ASSOCIATE Max Pellegrini,
max.pellegrini@dilbeck.com,
+1 626 584 0101
ON THE WEB Search for C59934

BREATHTAKING VIEWS
NEWPORT COAST, ORANGE COUNTY

- **Swimming pool and separate guest quarters**
- **Gated community with gym and tennis courts**

Overlooking the ocean and harbor lights on Crystal Cove's largest parcel, this impeccable gated residence offers the utmost privacy from which to enjoy some of the finest views in the state. Complementing the alluring vistas, the interior design details are equally impressive. Columns, archways, and rustic wood beams make soaring ceilings seem to stretch even

higher, while terracotta-tiled floors create a distinct sense of warmth. The main kitchen, living, and dining areas all flow outwards to expansive grounds framed by verdant mature landscaping. Here, a generous swimming pool, covered loggia, and secondary kitchen and outdoor cooking area can be found—ideally suited for hosting gatherings of any size. Four bedrooms include a master suite with sizeable walk-in closets and further mesmerizing ocean outlooks, the most impressive of which can be enjoyed from its tower with a private office and sitting areas. A luxurious ocean-view package, this glorious home is a Californian treasure.

OFFERED AT US$13,950,000
INQUIRIES **First Team Real Estate**, firstteam.com
ASSOCIATE Meital Taub, meital@taubproperties.com, +1 949 922 9552, taubproperties.com
ON THE WEB Search for C59881

CREE HOUSE
PALM SPRINGS AREA, RIVERSIDE COUNTY

- **An icon of Modernist architecture**
- **8.28-acre hillside site**
- **Fabulous outdoor entertaining space**

This iconic example of mid-century architecture was designed by Albert Frey—the master of what has become known as Desert Modernism. Following an exacting restoration, the stunning residence was revealed to the public for the first time during Modernism Week 2019. Painstaking efforts have been taken to preserve all the original building materials, including exterior and interior wall panels, superb fluted fiberglass deck pieces, kitchen appliances and cabinets, and even the glass shower door. Set on a hillside on 8.28 acres (3.3 ha), the property has a seamless connection with the outdoors thanks to expansive walls of glass, an enormous front deck, and a rear patio—all of which cleverly create a sense of the house extending beyond its own footprint. Built in harmony with the natural landscape, and boasting Frey's signature roof overhang, this jewel is a work of art, deserving of its place among the finest Modernist structures of all time.

OFFERED AT US$2,300,000
INQUIRIES HK Lane Real Estate, Inc.,
hklane.com
ASSOCIATES Andy Linsky,
Sven Vennen, and Kevin Bass,
ask@askpalmsprings.com,
+1 760 333 2228, forgottenfrey.com
ON THE WEB Search for C59849

LAKEFRONT DELIGHT
HOMEWOOD, PLACER COUNTY

- **Four bedrooms and three full baths**
- **Potential to build two new homes**
- **Prime location, close to amenities**

Available for the first time in almost 115 years, this lakefront legacy property boasts one of the best locations on the West Shore. Dating from 1906, the charming Old Tahoe residence spans 8,900 sq ft (827 sq m) with soaring ceilings, three bedrooms and three baths, an additional sleeping cabin, and a detached garage. Situated on a double lot of one acre (0.4 ha), it features 211 ft (64 m) of lake frontage and a stunning lakeside deck on which to relax and admire the views. The dwelling is well situated for some of Lake Tahoe's finest amenities, including the pristine shores and wonderful entertainment and dining opportunities. It is also just a short drive from Reno and Reno-Tahoe International Airport. With the potential to construct an additional two homes on the site, the acreage provides numerous options for development. This is a once-in-a-lifetime opportunity to own a unique estate on the polished stone shore of McKinney Bay in the heart of Homewood.

OFFERED AT US$8,995,000
INQUIRIES Oliver Luxury Real Estate Tahoe, oliverlux.com
ASSOCIATE Michael Oliver, michael@oliverlux.com, +1 530 525 6413
ON THE WEB Search for C59894

RESTFUL HIDEAWAY
TAHOMA, EL DORADO COUNTY

- **Four bedrooms and three full baths**
- **Plentiful leisure amenities**

This impressive three-story lakefront residence is located in an upscale gated complex within an unusually private area on the historic West Shore. Immaculately maintained, breathtaking details can be found throughout the dwelling, from the polished hardwood floors and superb wet bar, to granite countertops and a stunning island kitchen. High vaulted ceilings create an endless feeling of space, and an inviting stone fireplace in the first-floor living room provides a warm ambience. Outside, amenities include a swimming pool, a beautiful sandy beach, tennis courts, and a fabulous lakefront bar. A spacious wooden deck offers majestic views across the manicured grounds that run right to the water's edge, where, in addition to the use of a private pier, owners have access to exclusive buoys. These magnificent features combine to create the perfect place to entertain friends and family. This incredible luxury property presents a rare opportunity to own a waterfront home of such stature in this highly sought-after area.

OFFERED AT US$3,450,000
INQUIRIES Oliver Luxury Real Estate Tahoe, oliverlux.com
ASSOCIATE Darin Vicknair, darin@oliverlux.com, +1 530 308 2538
ON THE WEB Search for C59895

CALIFORNIA, UNITED STATES

COLORADO, UNITED STATES

PENTHOUSE PARADISE
ASPEN, PITKIN COUNTY

- **Impressive mountain panoramas**
- **Moments away from world-famous pistes**
- **Extensive indoor–outdoor living space**

This incredible penthouse has it all—a prime location close to skiing, upscale shopping, and Aspen Art Museum, plus breathtaking views. The property has been completely remodeled into a one-of-a-kind dream home. Built in 2008 and spanning 3,429 sq ft (318 sq m), the top-floor residence provides three bedrooms and

three-and-a-half baths. It also has a laundry room, office, underground two-car garage, and separate service entrance for added convenience. All systems, including the heating, ventilation, and air conditioning, have been replaced and only the highest-quality wood, stone, and wall treatments were utilized during the renovation. Fully automated with power blinds, shades, and drapes, the dwelling also has a Crestron system with easy one-touch control for music, light, and fireplaces. The pièce de résistance, however, is the spectacular mountain and park vistas that can be enjoyed from floor-to-ceiling windows and fabulous outdoor living spaces.

OFFERED AT US$21,950,000
INQUIRIES **Christie's International Real Estate**, christiesaspenre.com
ASSOCIATE Scott Davidson, scott@christiesaspenre.com, +1 970 948 4800
ON THE WEB Search for C60008

COLORADO, UNITED STATES

DOWNTOWN PERFECTION
ASPEN, PITKIN COUNTY

- Contemporary three-bedroom home
- South-facing decks with mountain views

This stunning, sun-drenched home blends modern living and a convenient downtown location with timeless Aspen Mountain vistas. Spacious living areas are spread over three stories, with the glorious scenery providing a picturesque backdrop to the 2,420 sq ft (225 sq m) floor plan. A superb upper level is characterized by high vaulted ceilings and skylights that flood the living room with light; a fully equipped fitted kitchen with a generous dining area; and an extensive south-facing deck. Each of the three bedrooms has its own bath, while the master suite also benefits from access to a deck. Supremely liveable, the residence is practical as well as stylish, boasting plentiful storage, a half bath, fireplaces, and a two-car garage. Nestled amid the trees, the property is located just two blocks from bustling City Market and four from Gondola Plaza, the heart of the town and the gateway to Aspen Mountain itself, making it both a perfect vacation retreat and a highly desirable year-round sanctuary.

OFFERED AT US$4,795,000
INQUIRIES Christie's International Real Estate, christiesaspenre.com
ASSOCIATE Joshua Landis, joshua@christiesaspenre.com, +1 970 948 9485
ON THE WEB Search for C59871

MOUNTAIN MAGIC

ASPEN, PITKIN COUNTY

- **Six bedrooms and six full baths**
- **More than 17 acres with spectacular views**

Panoramic mountain vistas are just the start of this elegant estate's appeal. Spanning more than 17 gently rolling acres (6.8 ha) with a large pond, waterfalls, mature trees, and beautiful landscaping, the property encompasses a five-bedroom main home and a three-car garage with staff accommodation. Sumptuous finishes and custom craftsmanship are in evidence throughout both levels of the primary house, including hardwood floors, inlaid-stone arches, beamed ceilings, and seven fireplaces. Most rooms offer sweeping views through floor-to-ceiling windows, and access to balconies or patios, for full appreciation of Independence Pass and the twin peaks that make up Mount Sopris. A gourmet kitchen accommodates top-of-the-line appliances, while the billiards room has a full wet bar and pool table. The opulent and spacious master suite includes an office, gym, walk-in closet, elevator access, and a full bath with fireplace, providing the finishing touches to this irresistible mountain residence.

OFFERED AT Price upon request
INQUIRIES **Christie's International Real Estate**, christiesaspenre.com
ASSOCIATE Scott Davidson, scott@christiesaspenre.com, +1 970 948 4800
ON THE WEB Search for C59936

COLORADO, UNITED STATES

TIMELESS ALPINE ELEGANCE
TELLURIDE, SAN MIGUEL COUNTY

• **Five-bedroom home in a spectacular setting**
• **Completely rebuilt in 2010**
• **Easy ski and golf access**

Exuding warmth and comfort, this elegantly appointed, five-bedroom, six-bath timber-and-stone home sits in an extraordinarily beautiful and completely private natural setting. Suitable for a growing family, but also perfect for large-scale entertaining, this stunning residence is surrounded by woods in an exclusive Mountain Village neighborhood. Completely rebuilt in 2010, the house now boasts the highest levels of finish and quality—interior stone, French limestone flooring, ceiling beams, and antique architectural pieces from Chateau Domingue combine harmoniously with walnut flooring, doors, and trim. Highlights include a gourmet kitchen with double Kohler sinks and a Viking stove, which opens to a patio, and a handsome dining room with generous windows capturing dramatic views of Campbell Peak. One of the few properties in the area to provide both ski and golf access, this exquisite dwelling offers style, tranquility, and incomparable luxury.

OFFERED AT US$4,985,000
INQUIRIES Telluride Real Estate Corp., gotelluride.com
ASSOCIATES Jon Dwight, jon@gotelluride.com, +1 970 708 0691, Alex Martin, alex@gotelluride.com, +1 970 729 1691, Marcin Ostromecki, marcin@gotelluride.com, +1 970 708 4119
ON THE WEB Search for C58456

LANDMARK PROPERTY
RIDGEFIELD, FAIRFIELD COUNTY

- **Spectacular residence and grounds**
- **Five acres featuring a private waterfall**

This almost 300-year-old gristmill—first used as a house in 1925 by paper magnate Nathaniel Miller—has been restored to an impressive standard to create one of the most remarkable properties in the area. Situated on five fenced acres (2 ha), it includes a 4,500 sq ft (418 sq m) main home overlooking a gorgeous waterfall, a large pond, a swimming pool, a guesthouse,

an office, and a boathouse. Considered to be a Ridgefield landmark, the historical primary residence also served as a cannonball factory during the Revolutionary War. Fully converted for residential use and benefiting from a recent five-year renovation, the magnificent interiors encompass three levels, including an intimate dining room that looks out over the water, an amazing two-story post-and-beam living room with a floor-to-ceiling stone fireplace, a wine cellar, and a spacious master suite. Add in the wealth of local history and the sounds of the waterfall in the background, and this dwelling is the ideal year-round or weekend retreat.

OFFERED AT US$3,495,000
INQUIRIES Neumann Real Estate, neumannrealestate.com
ASSOCIATE The Chip Neumann Team, cnt@neumannrealestate.com, +1 203 244 6077
ON THE WEB Search for C59959

SHORELINE CHARM
BRANFORD, NEW HAVEN COUNTY

- **Completely renovated turnkey property**
- **Year-round coastal paradise**
- **Tranquil water views**

Situated right on the tip of Haycock Point, between Indian Neck and the Pine Orchard area, is this stunning coastal cottage dating back to 1900. With unobstructed panoramic views, the home offers glorious sunrises over the Thimble Islands, romantic sunsets, and water vistas from every window. The house has been lovingly renovated, preserving all possible original details. Its spacious, open floor plan allows the interiors to be flooded with natural light and lets in the sounds of the peninsula, creating an inspiring and peaceful haven. A charming nautical theme has been impeccably maintained with exposed beams, vaulted ceilings, and wraparound porches. Surrounded by lapping waves and amazing bird life, the intimate seaside garden is a delight. By night, starry skies, meteor showers, and the distant twinkle of Long Island's lights dotting the horizon create a unique magical atmosphere in this superb waterfront sanctuary.

OFFERED AT US$2,400,000
INQUIRIES **Page Taft**, pagetaft.com
ASSOCIATE Lisa Pantalone Rollins,
lisa@rollinsgroupct.com,
+1 203 671 0295
ON THE WEB Search for C59844

BEACHFRONT OASIS

LOWER MATECUMBE KEY, MONROE COUNTY

- **Four-bedroom dream home**
- **Natural sandy beach and protected dockage**

Incredible sunrises across the Atlantic Ocean can be enjoyed each morning in this beautifully appointed residence, ideally located on a white sandy beach. The three-story luxury home is custom designed to capture the panoramic views of the shore and ocean. Floor-to-ceiling glass doors open on to tiled balconies featuring natural wood railings with clear glass inserts to capture the turquoise hues beyond. The open-flowing floor plan incorporates a large dining area conveniently located just off the gourmet kitchen for ease of entertaining. Three seating areas on the ground level, with keystone accent walls reminiscent of Florida's beautiful coral islands, are an idyllic place to relax. There is a separate guest bedroom wing, along with a private, third-level master suite. The location is perfect for walking along the crystal-clear waters of the shoreline, or spending the day on a boat, conveniently docked on the canalfront—with easy access to Florida Bay and the Atlantic Ocean.

OFFERED AT US$2,495,000

INQUIRIES **American Caribbean Real Estate**,
sales@americancaribbean.com,
+1 305 664 4966, +1 305 451 4078,
americancaribbean.com
ON THE WEB Search for C59900

FLORIDA, UNITED STATES

LUXURY CONDO LIVING
ST PETERSBURG, PINELLAS COUNTY

- **High-end customizations throughout**
- **Spectacular water and city views**

This custom three-bedroom, three-and-a-half bath corner condominium is located in one of the newest and most highly sought-after residential buildings in the area. Situated on the northeast side, the property boasts stunning views of Tampa Bay from the eastern balcony and city vistas from the den and guest suites. Floor-to-ceiling hurricane-impact windows flood the interiors with light, while motorized window shades come as part of a deluxe electronics package, and there is a vast array of designer extras. The pièce de résistance is the state-of-the-art chef's kitchen featuring a double-sized island with waterfall-effect granite, upgraded Wolf appliances, and a Sub-Zero refrigerator with double doors. Benefits of the incredible building include five-star amenities such as a 24-hour concierge service, valet parking, three owners' lounges, a large fitness center, a lap pool, a hot tub, grilling areas, and cabanas. Beautifully finished throughout, this is a luxury residence in a prime city location.

OFFERED AT US$2,200,000
INQUIRIES **Coastal Properties Group International, LLC**, coastalpgi.com
ASSOCIATE Liz Heinkel, lizheinkel@coastalpgi.com, +1 727 239 5623
ON THE WEB Search for C59868

PEACEFUL SANCTUARY

TRINITY, PASCO COUNTY

- **Four bedrooms and three-and-a-half baths**
- **Resort-like grounds with saltwater pool**

Custom designed and built to deliver the utmost in exclusive luxury living, this four-bedroom property is a prime offering. An impressive entryway with leaded glass doors introduces the home, in which every room is finished in immaculate style, with coffered ceilings, plantation shutters, graceful archways, and unique moldings complementing the high-end fixtures and finishes throughout. Dramatic, oversized windows immerse the interiors in natural light and offer beautiful panoramic views. In addition to a resplendent formal living room and superb dining room, a fabulous family space features an elegant dry bar and handsome fireplace, while a gourmet kitchen is characterized by opulent hardwood finishes and top-of-the-line stainless-steel appliances. The resort-like grounds boast a saltwater pool and heated spa, plus a well-equipped outdoor kitchen. Close to golfing, tennis, and further amenities, this stunning retreat is the epitome of fine Florida living.

OFFERED AT Price upon request
INQUIRIES **Coastal Properties Group International, LLC**, coastalpgi.com
ASSOCIATE Lori Crawford, ltcrawford01@aol.com, +1 727 234 8002
ON THE WEB Search for C59992

WATERFRONT MAJESTY

JUPITER ISLAND, MARTIN COUNTY

- **High-quality, impeccably styled interiors**
- **Amazing outdoor entertaining spaces**
- **Scenic views of the Intracoastal Waterway**

The epitome of luxurious waterfront living, this remarkable residence displays the finest craftsmanship throughout. Designed by Randall E Stofft Architects, the exceptional home comprises six bedrooms, six full baths, and two half baths, and has been impeccably maintained to illuminate the superb fixtures—handpicked from all over the world. Equally as memorable as the interior, the exteriors span more than an acre (0.67 ha) of meticulously landscaped grounds with abundant palms, dual summer kitchens, and an inviting infinity-edge pool and spa. Outdoor entertaining can be enjoyed beneath the pecky cypress ceiling of the expansive porch, with beautiful travertine floors and a soaring gas fireplace. Including approximately 162 ft (49 m) of picturesque Intracoastal Waterway, and a fully refurbished dock built to accommodate a large yacht plus a 16,000 lb (7,250 kg) lift for a smaller vessel, this is a prestigious property and a boater's dream.

OFFERED AT US$9,295,000
INQUIRIES **Fenton & Lang**,
fentonandlang.com
ASSOCIATE Joanne Wagner,
jwagner@fentonandlang.com,
+1 561 373 3127
ON THE WEB Search for C59937

WORLD-CLASS YACHT HAVEN

NORTH PALM BEACH, PALM BEACH COUNTY

- **14,000 sq ft modern villa**
- **Minutes from Palm Beach Inlet**

Sited on a rare double lot, this 14,000 sq ft (1,300 sq m) family home offers extraordinary privacy and serenity. A gated entry introduces the villa's landscaped 1.52-acre (0.6 ha) grounds, where ocean breezes and tropical sunsets can be enjoyed amid lush greenery. Custom built, the modern house provides grand-scale rooms that blend comfort and formality with design

elements such as Jerusalem stone and wood floors, custom millwork, and a masonry fireplace. A grand chef's kitchen opens on to sun-drenched family rooms—perfect for gatherings—while additional spaces include a gym, media room, office, and impressive 1,500-bottle wine cellar. Five bedrooms are complemented by a stunning master suite with grand lanai, and spacious double closets. The estate's private putting green with sand trap caters for golfers, while a boathouse with storage space, two docks capable of hosting superyachts, and easy ocean access make this offering the epitome of luxury waterside life.

OFFERED AT US$13,900,000
INQUIRIES Illustrated Properties Real Estate, Inc., ipre.com
ASSOCIATE Jennifer Hyland, hyland@ipre.com, +1 561 632 4042
ON THE WEB Search for C59787

PERFECT POSITION
SARASOTA, SARASOTA COUNTY

- Impeccably maintained four-bedroom home
- Peaceful position close to amenities
- Sweeping views of the beautiful shoreline

This incredible property occupies a desirable address within Harbor Acres. Surrounded by the area's most luxurious houses, it sits upon 160 ft (49 m) of waterfront close to the city lights of downtown, and with breathtaking panoramas of Bird Key. This impressive position offers a cornucopia of lush foliage and effortless indoor–outdoor entertaining. Originally built in 1954, the residence has since been totally renovated and pristinely maintained. Interior highlights include a chef's kitchen with adjacent breakfast room; a master retreat that takes in an expansive loft office, fabulous bath, and large walk-in closet; a media room or second master suite; and two guest bedrooms. Most rooms offer stunning views through Big Pass to the Gulf of Mexico, as well as Ringling Bridge and downtown. Pocket glass doors enhance the sublime vistas, and lead out to a screened lanai and pool terrace. Multiple garages with ample storage complete this beautiful estate.

OFFERED AT US$7,500,000
INQUIRIES Michael Saunders & Company, michaelsaunders.com
ASSOCIATE Kim Ogilvie, kimogilvie@michaelsaunders.com, +1 941 376 1717
ON THE WEB Search for C59956

PRIME LOCATION

PALM BEACH, PALM BEACH COUNTY

- Waterside position with breathtaking views
- Separate guest apartment with private entrance

Situated on almost half an acre (0.2 ha) on the Intracoastal Waterway, this landmark property boasts spectacular panoramic water views. Originally built in 1935, the five-bedroom, five full-bath home combines classical design, fine finishes, and custom millwork with an enviable North End location. The beautiful garden is an outdoor paradise with a covered loggia and gorgeous resort-style pool, plus a private dock with lift just across the Lake Trail. Breathtaking interiors span 5,283 sq ft (490 sq m) and deliver a host of luxury appointments. These include a cozy living room with marble fireplace; a formal dining room with French doors to the loggia; an island kitchen that opens to the family room and breakfast area; and a graceful circular staircase leading to an expansive master suite, three guest suites, and a sun terrace. Just steps from the water, this magnificent residence also offers easy access to boutiques, golf and tennis clubs, restaurants, museums, and galleries, as well as Palm Beach International Airport.

OFFERED AT US$11,850,000
INQUIRIES **Premier Estate Properties, Inc.,**
premierestateproperties.com
ASSOCIATE Rosalind Clarke,
rclarke@premierestateproperties.com,
+1 561 655 5570
ON THE WEB Search for C59882

FLORIDA, UNITED STATES

WATERSIDE LUXURY
LIGHTHOUSE POINT, BROWARD COUNTY

- Pool, tennis court, and dockage for a yacht
- Two separate guesthouses and a six-bay garage
- Impressive interiors ideal for entertaining

Nestled on 1.62 sublime acres (0.7 ha) of prime waterfront, facing the mansions of Hillsboro Mile, this palatial gated estate offers luxurious living at its finest, enhanced by a vast range of resort-style amenities. Ideal for avid boaters, the property includes 465 ft (141 m) of water frontage with 200 ft (61 m) of protected yacht dockage, just minutes from the Hillsboro Inlet. Spanning more than 15,000 sq ft (1,394 sq m), the primary residence is characterized by an array of grand entertaining spaces, as well as a stunning first-floor master wing with dual master baths, presenting the ultimate owners' retreat. The relaxing ocean breezes can be enjoyed from the beautiful verdant gardens, where two separate guesthouses provide further accommodation. Beyond the lure of the water, first-class amenities deliver endless leisure options in the form of a magnificent lighted tennis court, a sand volleyball court, a fitness center, and a lavish swimming pool.

OFFERED AT US$8,450,000
INQUIRIES **Premier Estate Properties, Inc.**,
premierestateproperties.com
ASSOCIATE Kevin Kreutzfeld,
kevin@premierestateproperties.com,
+1 954 449 7883
ON THE WEB Search for C59914

ISOLÉ VILLA
REUNION, OSCEOLA COUNTY

- **Contemporary design with 15 luxurious suites**
- **Impressive rental potential**

Located in Reunion Resort, just minutes from the region's theme parks, Isolé Villa is one of Orlando's premier vacation homes. A newly constructed masterpiece, it has 15 suites, 17 full baths, and six half baths within 23,000 sq ft (2,137 sq m) of indoor and outdoor living space. The majestic entrance dazzles with its two-story ceiling, and introduces a home

characterized by the finest furnishings and finishes. Entertaining is a breeze with a stunning contemporary kitchen and a separate catering kitchen, as well as a 40-seat formal dining area, board room, home theater, raised piano salon, and indoor basketball court. Elsewhere, a spa with a fitness center, massage room, steam room, sauna, and Zen lounge offers the ideal space to relax. Walls of sliding glass doors reveal an infinity-edge pool and Jacuzzi, plus a summer kitchen, bar, and numerous outdoor sitting areas. Zoned for short-term rental— by the day or week—the property offers the opportunity to generate significant income.

OFFERED AT US$9,750,000
INQUIRIES **Regal Real Estate**, regalrealtyorlando.com
ASSOCIATE Chris Christensen, chris@regalrealtyorlando.com, +1 407 312 8003
ON THE WEB Search for C59981

FLORIDA, UNITED STATES

EXCEPTIONAL CONDO
NAPLES, COLLIER COUNTY

- **Breathtaking water and park views**
- **Access to a private beach**
- **Stunning contemporary interiors**

Finesse and comfort meet modern elegance in this 4,548 sq ft (423 sq m) condominium, located in one of the most exclusive buildings in Naples. The open-flowing floor plan with floor-to-ceiling windows creates a harmonious balance between the indoor and outdoor areas —perfect for entertaining. A private elevator opens to the grand foyer of the immaculate apartment, which comprises three bedrooms and three-and-a-half stylish baths, plus a den. Residents can enjoy club-like amenities right on the doorstep, with two pools, a restaurant, a gym, and beach and poolside service delivering a five-star resort-style experience. In addition, there is access to a gorgeous private sugar-sand beach of more than 400 ft (122 m), and full-time security and concierge services are also provided. Beautiful contemporary interiors, breathtaking views, and an expansive array of impressive amenities make this incredible property the epitome of fine Florida living.

OFFERED AT US$4,900,000
INQUIRIES **William Raveis Real Estate**, raveis.com
ASSOCIATE John Paul Prebish, jp@raveis.com, +1 239 449 0254
ON THE WEB Search for C59835

GEORGIA, UNITED STATES

CLASSIC APPEAL
BUCKHEAD, ATLANTA

- **Delightful five-bedroom, five-bath estate**
- **Faithfully restored 1930s main home**
- **Tranquil gardens and swimming pool**

This handsome residence within an exclusive neighborhood is a tranquil retreat resting on 1.5 verdant acres (0.6 ha). Characterized by timeless details and a sensitive restoration, it easily combines architectural beauty with the comforts of a modern lifestyle. Originally built in 1938, the home's layout features a stunning conservatory addition, six fireplaces, a slate roof, copper gutters, and a pool with gazebo. The first floor provides a spacious living room with marble fireplace, a light-filled music room, a paneled library, a well-equipped kitchen, an airy dining room with French doors to access the pool and gazebo, and a family room with beverage center and fireplace opening to the soaring glass conservatory. A charming guest suite can also be found on the first floor, along with staff accommodation. Upstairs, the master suite enjoys a fireplace, vaulted bath, and dual closets, while two additional bedrooms and a recreation room complete this fabulous abode.

OFFERED AT Price upon request
INQUIRIES **Harry Norman, Realtors,** harrynorman.com
ASSOCIATE Studie Young, studie.young@harrynorman.com, +1 404 808 4142
ON THE WEB Search for C59957

HISTORIC ARCHITECTURE

COLUMBIA SQUARE, SAVANNAH

- **Remarkable six-bedroom mansion**
- **Beautifully preserved with modern updates**

This incredible property is one of the area's most celebrated Italianate mansions and was awarded the Historic Savannah Preservation Award in 2016. Built in 1884, it is now one of the premier estates on resplendent Columbia Square. Heritage details, including original Kehoe Iron Works metalcrafts, are intact both inside and out, yet no modern comfort or amenity has been overlooked in the renovation of this six-bedroom, seven-bath residence. A vast array of stunning light-filled living spaces open to iron balconies and a charming rooftop terrace that is built with entertaining in mind. State-of-the-art mechanical systems and security can be found throughout, including an elevator that serves all floors. A superbly appointed carriage house offers separate guest accommodation or could be used for rental income. The property also includes a highly coveted two-car garage at street level and recent restorations have been made for the long-term preservation of this architectural treasure.

OFFERED AT Price upon request
INQUIRIES Seabolt Brokers, LLC,
seaboltbrokers.com
ASSOCIATE Elaine Seabolt,
eseabolt@seaboltbrokers.com,
+1 912 224 7511
ON THE WEB Search for C59899

THE SULLIVAN ESTATE
HALEIWA, HONOLULU COUNTY

- **Park-like grounds overlooking the North Shore**
- **Just 50 minutes from Honolulu**

This magnificent estate provides an unrivaled opportunity to live like a star. Currently operating as a luxury wellness spa that has been a haven for icons such as Elvis Presley and U2's Bono, potential abounds at The Sullivan Estate. The collection of structures overlooks 15 miles (24 km) of the North Shore of Oahu from five picturesque acres (2 ha). From the

Pupukea plateau, the lush grounds cascade down towards the sea-level plains below, with incredible views taking in Waimea Bay and the mountain ranges of West Oahu. Walkways and pools join the accommodations woven through the park-like grounds, and guests can relax in serene quarters that characterize the property's alluring appeal. Beautifully maintained, the compound could readily shift from spa retreat to a private sanctuary, or be subdivided into separate homes. With easy access to the North Shore's world-renowned surf breaks, location is key—the estate's majesty enhanced by the natural environment surrounding it.

OFFERED AT US$19,800,000
INQUIRIES Hawaii Life Real Estate Brokers, hawaiilife.com
ASSOCIATE Sean Ginella, seanginella@hawaiilife.com, +1 808 372 8700
ON THE WEB Search for C59343

HAWAII, UNITED STATES

COASTAL BEAUTY

LAHAINA, MAUI

- A rare 3.5 acres of waterfront land
- Stunning unobstructed views of the ocean

One of Maui's most majestic properties, this unique offering sits on a secluded oceanfront promontory known as the Alaelae Peninsula. Sited on 3.5 acres (1.4 ha), the residence is just a short distance from the heart of Kapalua Resort, DT Fleming Beach, and the world-renowned surfing spot of Honolua Bay. Beyond a set of fabulous custom gates, a driveway leads through the mature landscaping of the estate's beautiful grounds. The location is breathtaking, with striking views of the Pacific Ocean and the island of Moloka'i, plus—in season—the sight of humpback whales breaching the waves by the peninsula. Situated in a conservation area, which limits surrounding development, the single-level home contains four bedrooms, including a lavish master suite with expansive walk-in closet. Delivering the utmost privacy and panoramic, unobstructed vistas of the water, this is an enviable dwelling providing the finest in relaxed luxury living on a rarely available, larger-than-average oceanfront plot.

OFFERED AT US$9,900,000
INQUIRIES **Hawaii Life Real Estate Brokers**, soldmaui.com
ASSOCIATE Mary Anne Fitch, sold@maui.net, +1 808 250 1583
ON THE WEB Search for C59862

MOUNTAIN ECO-HOME
SUN VALLEY, BLAINE COUNTY

- **Custom log-built home**
- **Classic Sun Valley Fairway location**
- **Eco-friendly improvements**

This custom residence encompasses numerous green initiatives without compromising on its awe-inspiring contemporary mountain style. Montana logs, milled onsite; Italian plastered interior walls; and reclaimed chestnut floors from a Civil War-era bridge characterize the superb interiors. Built with the environment in mind, its amenities include solar-heated water and 80 percent solar-powered utilities. With five spacious bedrooms and three-and-a-half baths, this is both a beautiful and functional family dwelling. The primary level boasts an open-flowing floor plan, with abundant light, three fireplaces, and a large master suite, plus a generous kitchen with a center island and cherry cabinets, while the exterior features an outdoor fireplace for nights under the stars, as well as a vast vegetable garden. A solar-heated Jacuzzi and Himalayan salt sauna are further highlights, while the amazing location near Sun Valley Lodge completes the incredible package.

OFFERED AT US$4,050,000
**INQUIRIES Sun Valley Real Estate
LLC,** sunvalleyrealestate.com
ASSOCIATE Suzanne Williams,
suzannesunvalley@gmail.com,
+1 208 720 3951
ON THE WEB Search for C59974

GULL'S ROCK

NORTHEAST HARBOR, HANCOCK COUNTY

- **A total of nine bedrooms**
- **Picturesque setting**

Located on the majestic shores of Great Harbor, Gull's Rock boasts a coveted position in an exclusive enclave. The classic nine-bedroom residence has been beautifully maintained, and has undergone a contemporary and thoughtful restoration—updating its appeal and ensuring that the busy lives of modern families can be accommodated. All first-floor rooms have generous fireplaces and several also provide easy access to the open or covered porches that overlook the colorful English-style perennial garden. A grand chef's kitchen offers an array of gourmet fixtures, including a center island, high-end professional appliances, and a large butler's pantry. There is a separate three-car garage, which houses two additional rooms and a full bath, while a guest cabin has two bedrooms and a full bath. A short stroll through the sumptuous grounds reveals panoramic vistas over the stunning ocean shoreline, emphasizing the picturesque qualities of this exceptional property.

OFFERED AT US$6,750,000
INQUIRIES LandVest, Inc.,
landvest.com
ASSOCIATE Story Litchfield,
slitchfield@landvest.com,
+1 207 276 3840
ON THE WEB Search for C59953

MARYLAND, UNITED STATES

CASA INALA

EDGEWATER, ANNE ARUNDEL COUNTY

- **Five bedrooms and six-and-a-half baths**
- **Supremely peaceful and private**

Situated on more than three acres (1.2 ha) in a highly prestigious area, this superb waterfront masterpiece affords unrivaled tranquility and luxury. Panoramas of the South River abound from the nearly 7,000 sq ft (650 sq m) Spanish Colonial-inspired estate. Steeped in Maryland history, Casa Inala sits in what was once called Londontowne, a major hub for travelers in the late 1600s to early 1800s. Historic Scott Street can still be seen winding alongside the home, and the William Brown House—a National Historic Landmark—is located on an adjacent lot. Premium fixtures can be found in the gourmet kitchen, while five bedrooms and six-and-a-half baths are the epitome of luxury and comfort. With a prime waterfront location, the estate boasts pristinely landscaped gardens, 300 ft (91 m) of water frontage with a sandy beach, and a 300 ft (91 m) dock. The setting can be enjoyed from the pool and hot tub, or from the Agassi Tower, where 360-degree vistas take in the river and the passing of migratory birds.

OFFERED AT US$5,000,000
INQUIRIES Long & Foster Real Estate, Inc., longandfoster.com
ASSOCIATE Todd Werling, todd.werling@longandfoster.com, +1 240 497 1700
ON THE WEB Search for C59924

WATERFRONT RETREAT
CROWNSVILLE, ANNE ARUNDEL COUNTY

- **Eight-bedroom showcase residence**
- **Secluded area with good transport links**
- **Landscaped grounds and private boat dock**

A gated entrance introduces Homestead on the Severn, an enclave of refined estate homes just minutes from major commuting routes. This stone-and-cedar, custom-built residence comes with every amenity and comfort imaginable. There is more than 150 ft (46 m) of riprapped shoreline and a deep-water, multislip pier with boatlifts, plus delightful landscaping and night lighting. The luxurious main living level of the eight-bedroom property has a superb gourmet kitchen, plus an outdoor kitchen, and a master retreat with en suite bath and dual walk-in closets. Downstairs, a finished walk-out lower level delivers a temperature-controlled wine cellar, a home theater, a steam room, and a wet bar. High-end finishes such as coffered ceilings, exquisite trim and moldings, and sumptuous fireplaces appear throughout the house, and a cherry-paneled elevator connects the floors. No detail has been overlooked in this elegant and beautifully equipped waterfront property.

OFFERED AT US$3,900,000
INQUIRIES **Long & Foster Real Estate, Inc.**, longandfoster.com
ASSOCIATE Lori Gough, lori.gough@longandfoster.com, +1 410 224 0600
ON THE WEB Search for C59925

STATELY FLAIR
POTOMAC, MONTGOMERY COUNTY

- **Custom home with elegant interiors**
- **Beautiful outdoor living space with pool**

Located in the sought-after area of Falconhurst, this vast custom-built stone manor house is magnificent. A show-stopping two-story foyer with dramatic staircase introduces the superb interiors, where soaring ceilings and walls of windows fill every room with natural light. Particularly of note is the double-height family room, which boasts a stone-accented fireplace, while the chef's kitchen is also impeccable with custom cabinets, concrete countertops, and high-end appliances. The first floor hosts a luxurious master suite with sitting room and spa-like baths, and five additional bedrooms in the main home all include their own bath and large walk-in closets. A charming guesthouse could accommodate visitors or be used as staff quarters. The 5,000 sq ft (465 sq m) basement has immaculate exercise facilities, as well as a generous entertaining area with bar. Outside, flagstone terraces are accompanied by a pool and spa, and a tennis court, offering endless leisure opportunities in an idyllic gated setting.

OFFERED AT US$4,100,000
INQUIRIES **Long & Foster Real Estate, Inc.**, longandfoster.com
ASSOCIATE Jennifer Chow, jennifer.chow@longandfoster.com, +1 301 213 5364
ON THE WEB Search for C59926

THE UNITED TALENTS OF

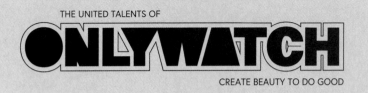

ONLYWATCH

CREATE BEAUTY TO DO GOOD

9 NOVEMBER 2019 - 2PM, GENEVA

A BIENNIAL CHARITY AUCTION OF UNIQUE TIMEPIECES
FOR RESEARCH ON DUCHENNE MUSCULAR DYSTROPHY

Participants as per July 16, 2019

WORLD TOUR EXHIBITION

MONACO, SEP. 25-28 | DUBAI, OCT. 1-3 | PARIS, OCT. 7-8 | LONDON, OCT. 11-13 | NEW YORK, OCT. 16-17
TOKYO, OCT. 23-24 | SINGAPORE, OCT. 25-26 | HONG KONG, OCT. 28-29 | TAIPEI, OCT. 30-31 | GENEVA, NOV. 7-9

Organised by

Auctioned by

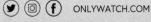

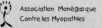 Association Monégasque
Contre les Myopathies

CHRISTIE'S

BESPOKE LUXURY
MONOMOY, NANTUCKET

- **Picturesque coastal location**
- **Stunning independent guesthouse**

Designed with lavish family living in mind, this bespoke estate is the epitome of modern luxury. Situated within extensive grounds, it comprises a main residence, superb guesthouse, and two-car garage with self-contained studio. Meticulously finished throughout, the primary home is the picture of timeless elegance. The first floor features a gorgeous kitchen that opens into a casual living space with handsome barrel ceiling, a heavenly master suite with a fabulous soaking tub and sitting area, a wet bar with wine storage, and several access points to the outdoor terrace that looks out to the pool and manicured gardens. On the second floor, a TV room with balcony overlooking the pool, and a second master suite with ample walk-in closets and an opulent bath can be found, along with three additional bedrooms. A beautiful staircase leads up to the third floor and the incredible widow's walk—a rooftop retreat with magnificent vistas of the harbor, which can also be enjoyed from the front balcony.

OFFERED AT US$8,995,000
INQUIRIES Great Point Properties, Inc., greatpointproperties.com
ASSOCIATE Bill Liddle, bill@greatpointproperties.com, +1 508 228 2266
ON THE WEB Search for C59985

RED GATE FARM
AQUINNAH, MARTHA'S VINEYARD

- **340-acre (138 ha) oceanfront estate**
- **Large Cape Cod-style house with coastal views**

Situated in a wonderfully remote area, this sprawling legacy estate represents a natural oceanfront sanctuary, once the cherished summer home of Jacqueline Kennedy Onassis. The picture of timeless elegance, the cedar-shingled residence was originally designed by renowned architect Hugh Newell Jacobsen, and renovated by Deborah Berke, dean of the Yale School of Architecture. On the primary level, a formal sitting room with fireplace, a drawing room, and an expansive chef's kitchen all deliver stunning views of the Atlantic, and two decks present breathtaking vistas across the dunes. Upstairs, four bedrooms include a sumptuous master suite, while an intimate den, two offices/art studios, and a basement are also highlights. The four-bedroom, three-bath Shingle-style guesthouse adds further charm. With more than a mile of private beachfront, two freshwater ponds, a pool, and a tennis court, this alluring compound offers a multitude of luxury amenities with superb surroundings.

OFFERED AT US$65,000,000
INQUIRIES LandVest, Inc.,
landvest.com;
Christie's International Real Estate,
christiesrealestate.com
ASSOCIATES Gerret Conover,
gcc@mvlandvest.com,
+1 508 627 1617, Tom LeClair,
tel@mvlandvest.com,
+1 508 627 3757; Kathleen Coumou,
kcoumou@christies.com,
+1 212 974 4592
ON THE WEB Search for C59865

MASSACHUSETTS, UNITED STATES

RELAXING FAMILY ESTATE
HARWICH PORT, BARNSTABLE COUNTY

• **Eight bedrooms and seven-and-a-half baths**
• **Impressive resort-style grounds**

This unparalleled family estate is built with luxurious outdoor living in mind, boasting 5.8 acres (2.3 ha) of meticulously landscaped grounds with a two-hole golf range, clay tennis court, heated pool with cabana, and hot tub. The home extends over 6,764 sq ft (628 sq m) of living space with impressive dual staircases in the foyer. A state-of-the-art kitchen with full-service butler's pantry opens to a great room, while a living room, library, en suite bedroom, laundry, and shower room complete the level. Upstairs, a sitting room with fireplace and balcony is flanked by two sumptuous master suites, a further bedroom, and a study accessed by its own stairway. A lower level encompasses plenty of leisure space, with a home theater, billiards room, exercise room, sauna, and wine room, plus an eight-car garage. Visitors can enjoy privacy in a four-bedroom guesthouse complete with a magnificent great room and kitchen facilities. Below it lies a three-car garage stocked with equipment for sports fishing.

OFFERED AT US$5,495,000
INQUIRIES **Pine Acres Realty**, pineacresrealty.com
ASSOCIATE Chris Rhinesmith, chris@pineacresrealty.com, +1 508 945 1186
ON THE WEB Search for C59888

MICHIGAN, UNITED STATES

CONTEMPORARY REFINEMENT
BLOOMFIELD TOWNSHIP, OAKLAND COUNTY

- Situated on almost one acre (0.4 ha)
- Sumptuous master suite

Recently renovated to the highest standards, this stunning estate marries classic features with contemporary style. The expansive grounds form a tranquil sanctuary with a gorgeous bluestone patio for relaxing and entertaining. Inside, the open and flexible floor plan allows the living space to be personalized. High-end finishes can be enjoyed throughout, with Brazilian cherry floors punctuating the elegant design. An open kitchen and family room, intimate nook/office, and eat-in breakfast area provide ample living space. A sublime master suite extends along an entire wing of the house with a luxurious master bath and brand-new walk-in closet with center island. Each of the home's bedrooms comes with its own bath and extensive closet space. Completing the property is an oversized six-car garage tall enough for a car lift, adding enormous appeal for a collector. Alternatively, a portion of this space could be converted to create additional living areas, a recreation room/gym, or a teen oasis.

OFFERED AT Price upon request
INQUIRIES Hall & Hunter Realtors,
hallandhunter.com
ASSOCIATE Sam Kaplunov,
sam@hallandhunter.com,
+1 248 933 0471
ON THE WEB Search for C59902

CLASSIC HILLTOP HOME
MANISTEE, MANISTEE COUNTY

- Three acres with spectacular views
- Four bedrooms and five full baths
- Development potential

This stunning 1940s residence boasts an idyllic setting on a three-acre (1.21 ha) hilltop plot in Manistee's old town, with incredible Lake Michigan views and sunsets. Classic in every sense, the estate benefits from a park-like setting with beautifully landscaped grounds and multiple outdoor living spaces including expansive decks, patios, and an outdoor sauna. Meticulously maintained throughout, and providing an array of modern upgrades, the home features four bedrooms, five-and-a-half baths, a large bonus room, a studio apartment with another bedroom and bath above the garage, and a partially finished basement. The large parcel can be split into three separate lots, all with Lake Michigan vistas, offering exciting development potential. Just a five-minute walk to the beach, restaurants, and the Manistee Pierhead Lighthouse, this property could be the perfect family retreat, used as a B&B, or transformed to suit individual needs.

OFFERED AT Price upon request
INQUIRIES **North Harbor Real Estate**, northharborrealestate.com
ASSOCIATE Lora Higdon, jay-lora@northharborrealestate.com, +1 734 626 0969
ON THE WEB Search for C59915

MICHIGAN, UNITED STATES

BLISSFUL LAKESIDE CABIN
EVERGREEN POINT, CHARLEVOIX COUNTY

• Fabulous surroundings with extensive views
• Soaring, double-height entertaining spaces

Located just steps from Lake Charlevoix, charm and luxury are in abundance at this splendid three-bedroom hideaway. The fabulous main floor boasts a soaring living and entertaining space, with a two-story stone fireplace and hardwood floors. Custom design and superb finishes delight throughout the home, with its elegant granite kitchen, expansive games room, spacious master suite, and impressive exercise room with breathtaking views overlooking the lake. A sizeable pole barn offers a wood shop and workout room, and provides the property with plenty of storage. Outside the house, a generous covered front porch is the perfect place to relax with stunning vistas over the 200 ft (61 m) of private waterfront. Two acres (0.8 ha) of mature, professional landscaping are complemented by a vast rolling lawn, waterfall, and stream, and an exclusive 40 ft (12 m) pier— suitable for any size of yacht—is an ideal fit for Lake Charlevoix's natural harbor and makes exploring the surrounding beauty a breeze.

OFFERED AT US$3,800,000
INQUIRIES **North Harbor Real Estate**, northharborrealestate.com
ASSOCIATE Jeff Wellman, jeff@northharborrealestate.com, +1 231 675 9892
ON THE WEB Search for C59916

MONTANA, UNITED STATES

DESIGN PERFECTION
BOZEMAN, GALLATIN COUNTY

- **Spectacular scenic views**
- **Extensive outdoor facilities**
- **Adjacent 20-acre (8 ha) parcel also for sale**

Characterized by breathtaking panoramas and magnificent living spaces, this incredible three-bedroom residence is an entertainer's dream. The flowing floor plan faces north, with expansive glass doors and windows drawing the outdoors in. Leisure opportunities abound, with a home theater and wine cellar, as well as a gourmet kitchen featuring three different dining areas and a two-sided fireplace. The 21-acre (8.5 ha) estate boasts beautifully maintained gardens, a pond, a lake, captivating waterfalls, a golf driving range, an archery range, and a plunge pool, as well as a fully appointed three-bedroom guesthouse. Superb outdoor entertaining spaces encompass luxurious amenities such as a wood-burning fireplace, a firepit, heated dining areas, and surround sound throughout to conjure an enviable ambience. Designed with comfort and opulence in mind, this property delivers every convenience in a highly sought-after position.

OFFERED AT Price upon request
INQUIRIES PureWest Real Estate,
purewestrealestate.com
ASSOCIATE Mike Schlauch,
mike@suplatinum.com,
+1 406 580 8380
ON THE WEB Search for C55219

STYLISH FAMILY HOME
RUMSON, MONMOUTH COUNTY

• **Five-bedroom home with luxurious amenities**
• **Close to the beach and links to Manhattan**

Beautifully designed, this stunning Southern-inspired residence has been built to the highest standards, boasting handcrafted cedar shake exteriors, and dazzling custom millwork and coffered ceilings within. Nestled in resort-like grounds, with a gorgeous pool with swim-up bar, an outdoor fireplace, and cabana, the home delivers impressive outdoor living to match the superb interiors. The contemporary layout creates the perfect space for both casual family living and large-scale entertaining. A gourmet kitchen features high-end appliances and exquisite cabinetry, and opens out into a remarkable double-height family room. On the second floor, four bedrooms are joined by a grand master suite with a fireplace and sitting area, along with a magnificent covered porch. Within the finished basement, a home theater, gym, and wine cellar complete the desirable amenities of this luxury property, conveniently located just minutes from wonderful beaches and the high-speed ferry to Manhattan.

OFFERED AT US$3,999,000
INQUIRIES Gloria Nilson & Co. Real Estate, glorianilson.com
ASSOCIATE Mario Venancio, mvenancio@glorianilson.com, +1 732 530 2800
ON THE WEB Search for C59942

SOPHISTICATED LIVING
RUMSON, MONMOUTH COUNTY

Elegance and warmth unite in this exquisitely renovated home located on 3.88 acres (1.57 ha) with a pool, spa, pool house, tennis court, and carriage house. Luxury appointments can be found throughout, particularly in the sublime master suite with two fireplaces, a sitting room, and stunning master bath.

OFFERED AT US$4,500,000
INQUIRIES **Gloria Nilson & Co. Real Estate**, glorianilson.com
ASSOCIATE Gloria Nilson, gnilson@glorianilson.com, +1 732 842 6009
ON THE WEB Search for C59946

RIVERFRONT GEM
RED BANK, MONMOUTH COUNTY

Sunset views can be enjoyed from almost every room of this stunning residence. An open-plan layout is ideal for family living and entertaining, while four bedrooms include a luxury master suite with terrace. Pristine grounds lead to a deep-water dock and boatlift, completing the package.

OFFERED AT US$2,825,000
INQUIRIES **Gloria Nilson & Co. Real Estate**, glorianilson.com
ASSOCIATE Mario Venancio, mvenancio@glorianilson.com, +1 732 530 2800
ON THE WEB Search for C59944

ARCHITECTURAL MASTERPIECE
COLTS NECK, MONMOUTH COUNTY

Situated in a 2.5-acre (1 ha) wooded setting, this custom home exudes timeless beauty. Natural hardwood floors, French doors, coffered ceilings, and detailed moldings adorn the opulent interiors, and all four bedrooms are en suite. A home theater, wet bar, and bonus room on the lower level are ideal for entertaining.

OFFERED AT US$2,395,000
INQUIRIES **Gloria Nilson & Co. Real Estate**, glorianilson.com
ASSOCIATE Catherine Erkal, cerkal@glorianilson.com, +1 732 946 3200
ON THE WEB Search for C59943

SEASONAL MAJESTY
PRINCETON, MERCER COUNTY

High ceilings, large windows, and an open floor plan define this expansive four-bedroom residence. A bespoke Bulthaup kitchen and two luxurious master suites are interior highlights, while outside there is an extensive mahogany deck and supremely private landscaped grounds surrounded by majestic trees.

OFFERED AT US$2,100,000
INQUIRIES **Gloria Nilson & Co. Real Estate**, glorianilson.com
ASSOCIATE Alison Covello, acovello@glorianilson.com, +1 609 921 2600
ON THE WEB Search for C59745

DESIGN EXCELLENCE
SANTA FE, SANTA FE COUNTY

- **Breathtaking interiors**
- **Tranquil environment**
- **Mountain views**

Clean lines, soaring ceilings, and plenty of natural light combine to create a remarkable, contemporary living space in this impressive residence. Located just a mile from downtown Santa Fe, the property is accessed via a circular driveway, which introduces the private, serene environment with stone steps leading up to

the gated courtyard entry. Upon entering the dwelling, the dramatic open-concept design, created by noted architect John Klee, delivers a sophisticated yet informal living area. Walls of glass offer spectacular views of the Sandia mountains. The opposite wing of the home includes a library, guest bedroom, and exquisite master suite with sitting area and its own terrace. Connecting the two is a delightful patio, equally suited for moments of quiet reflection or entertaining in Santa Fe style. Elsewhere, an attached guesthouse/studio and a two-car garage complete this breathtaking offering set in a landscape of mature trees.

OFFERED AT US$1,195,000
INQUIRIES Barker Realty, Inc.,
santaferealestate.com
ASSOCIATE John Hancock,
jhancock@santaferealestate.com,
+1 505 470 5604
ON THE WEB Search for C59861

GRACIOUS TOWNHOUSE
UPPER WEST SIDE, MANHATTAN

- Six bedrooms and seven baths
- South-facing garden and roof terrace
- Prime position in a tree-lined historic district

One of six original Victorian brownstones in a sought-after area, this four-story townhouse was built in 1893 and has been completely restored to its original splendor. On entry, a wood-paneled foyer with oak flooring and an intricately carved staircase leads to a well-equipped kitchen and a bedroom with garden access. The centerpiece of the next level is a bright living room with chandeliers, a wet bar, and superb views of the historic district. This story also includes a formal dining room with a fireplace; an ample eat-in kitchen; and stairs down to the garden. The third floor comprises a spacious master suite with original hardwood floors, a fireplace, and a spa-like marble bath, plus space for a study or library, while further bedrooms on the fourth floor open to a rooftop terrace for vistas of the Hudson River. A perfect marriage of modernity and period charm, the home also features a large finished basement and a new air-conditioning system.

OFFERED AT US$7,995,000
INQUIRIES **Christie's International Real Estate Group**, christiesrealestate.com
ASSOCIATE Edward F Joseph, ejoseph@christies.com, +1 212 974 4434
ON THE WEB Search for C59998

NEW YORK, UNITED STATES

NEW YORK, UNITED STATES

MAGNIFICENT CONDO
UPPER EAST SIDE, MANHATTAN

- **Five bedrooms and seven-and-a-half baths**
- **Noted address close to Central Park**

A private elevator with white-glove service leads to this five-bedroom residence in a celebrated 1940s condominium. On arrival, a welcoming foyer flows into a light-filled entertaining wing with south-facing windows. The space includes a large living and dining room; an eat-in island kitchen with stainless-steel Miele appliances; a corner library or guest room with a full bath; and a butler's pantry and staff area with its own entrance and a half bath. On the other side of the foyer is the secluded master suite, which boasts windows on three sides, a trio of walk-in closets, a dressing room, and dual marble baths with heated floors. Three more spacious bedrooms all feature en suite baths, ample sunlight, and generous walk-in closets. Superb detailing and high-quality materials throughout the home take in solid oak floors, custom windows, marble countertops, and aluminum cabinetry. The grand building itself sits just moments from Central Park, first-rate restaurants, and world-renowned shopping.

OFFERED AT US$14,495,000
INQUIRIES Christie's International Real Estate Group, The Erin Boisson Aries Team, christiesrealestate.com
ASSOCIATES Erin Boisson Aries, earies@christies.com, +1 212 974 4551, Nic Bottero, nbottero@christies.com, +1 212 636 2638
ON THE WEB Search for C59999

NEW YORK, UNITED STATES

NEW YORK, UNITED STATES

AWE-INSPIRING CONVERSION
WEST CHELSEA, MANHATTAN

- **Dramatic original architecture**
- **Garden and potential for expansion**

Extraordinary light and scale abound in this converted warehouse, where an awe-inspiring exposed-brick living space spans more than 6,400 sq ft (595 sq m). Ceilings soar to over 30 ft (9 m), showcasing original wooden beams from the building's days as a production and art studio for Broadway sets. With both first-floor and parlor-level entrances, this property is configured perfectly for an artist, gallerist, or collector. Meticulously restored and modernized, the residence flows across four levels, under double- and triple-height ceilings, all connected by a series of striking stairs and bridges. Light pours in through skylights and a wall of windows, while an expansive terrace and 750 sq ft (70 sq m) garden with 22 ft-high (6.7 m-high) walls provide equally impressive outdoor space. With vibrant West Chelsea at the center of the Hudson River and Downtown Manhattan development boom, this property is a sensational marriage between authentic old New York and the dynamic 21st-century city.

OFFERED AT US$18,500,000
INQUIRIES **Christie's**
International Real Estate Group,
The Erin Boisson Aries Team
christiesrealestate.com
ASSOCIATES Erin Boisson Aries,
earies@christies.com,
+1 212 974 4551, Nic Bottero,
nbottero@christies.com,
+1 212 636 2638, Dustin Crouse,
dcrouse@christies.com,
+1 212 636 2234
ON THE WEB Search for C59807

NEW YORK, UNITED STATES

HISTORICAL MANSION
UPPER EAST SIDE, MANHATTAN

- Five bedrooms and six full baths
- Fully updated Modernist masterpiece

An architectural tour de force in a coveted location, this iconic property was one of the first Modernist townhouses in Manhattan. Commissioned by inventor and investor Sherman M Fairchild, the home was designed to match his adventurous spirit, and completed in 1941. The building's 25 ft-wide (7.6 m-wide) minimalist façade hints at the postmodern wonders inside, where striking ramps zigzag their way through the light-filled home, weaving the 9,440 sq ft (877 sq m) interior together. The result is an airy interpretation of a traditional townhouse and the perfect setting for an art collection. Highlights include a three-story great room, its travertine walls illuminated by a glass-and-steel skylight, and a master suite boasting two baths and a balcony. A gourmet kitchen, formal dining room, study/library, wine cellar, and an additional four bedrooms—one a light-infused loft—complete this one-of-a-kind offer. With Central Park and Museum Mile on its doorstep, this is a home unlike any other.

OFFERED AT US$35,000,000
INQUIRIES Christie's International Real Estate Group,
christiesrealestate.com
ASSOCIATE Kathleen Coumou,
kcoumou@christies.com,
+1 212 468 7140
ON THE WEB Search for C59353

MEMPHIS DOWNTOWN
WEST VILLAGE, MANHATTAN

- Three units on two floors
- Prime location with 360-degree views
- Direct elevator access

Rising high above the West Village skyline, this one-of-a-kind proposition includes three apartment units, which can either be combined to create one luxury duplex condominium, kept separate, or developed as a combination of the two. An ambitious architectural conversion reimagines these spaces as an open-plan home with 4,280 sq ft (397 sq m) of living space, and some 750 sq ft (70 sq m) of outdoor space. The units offer panoramic views of the Hudson River to the west, the Statue of Liberty to the south, the Empire State Building to the north, and an uninterrupted New York cityscape to the east. Building amenities include a 24-hour concierge and a parking garage with direct access via elevator to the apartments. Nearby are the Whitney Museum of Art, Hudson River Park, the High Line, Chelsea Arts District, and enough shops to satisfy all tastes, along with some of the best restaurants in New York City.

OFFERED AT US$9,995,000
INQUIRIES Christie's International Real Estate Group,
christiesrealestate.com
ASSOCIATE Edward F Joseph,
ejoseph@christies.com,
+1 212 974 4434
ON THE WEB Search for C59736

NEW YORK, UNITED STATES

URBAN OASIS

BATTERY PARK CITY, MANHATTAN

- **Surrounded by parks and leisure amenities**
- **Full-time concierge, doorman, and porter**

Defined by a superb sense of space, this pristine two-bedroom, two-bath apartment in the grand Visionaire condominium is a sleek and stylish sanctuary with a multitude of shopping, dining, and sporting facilities at its doorstep. The home boasts soaring ceilings, oversized windows to make the most of the incredible vistas, wooden floors, and high-end amenities—from black granite countertops in the kitchen to custom-built closets and a marble bath. Within the building itself, communal spaces and services are on hand for every occasion. Sunset views of the Hudson River can be enjoyed from the Sky Lounge, which also provides a barbecue and wet bar; a residents' lounge is an intimate retreat with its large-screen TV and fireplace; and a gym, fitness classes, and a 50 ft (15 m) pool deliver plentiful leisure options. The LEED Platinum-certified property also uses the latest air filtration, solar, and geothermal technologies to create an environmentally friendly space in the heart of Battery Park City.

OFFERED AT US$2,450,000
INQUIRIES **Christie's International Real Estate Group**, christiesrealestate.com
ASSOCIATES Herbert Chou, hchou@christies.com, +1 212 468 7118, Natalya Bowen, nbowen@christies.com. +1 212 974 4411
ON THE WEB Search for C60010

GRAND VICTORIAN MANSION
SOUTH NYACK, ROCKLAND COUNTY

Luxury living space defines
this fully restored Victorian
mansion, situated on the
banks of the Hudson River.
The six-bedroom home boasts
high-quality finishes and
amenities including marble
floors, granite countertops,
and wood-burning fireplaces,
plus a gunite pool, two gyms,
and a projection room.

OFFERED AT US$4,500,000
INQUIRIES **Christie's International
Real Estate Westchester and Hudson
Valley**, christiesrehudsonvalley.com
ASSOCIATE David Sanders,
david@sandershomes.com,
+1 845 304 3344
ON THE WEB Search for C60004

GLENHOLME
UPPER NYACK, ROCKLAND COUNTY

Exhilarating Hudson River
views, wide lawns, and a
cascading brook set the tone
of this six-bedroom, five-bath
estate. Extensively renovated,
highlights of the breathtaking
interiors include a living room
with a fireplace and French
doors, and a gracious dining
room with a secret passage to
the gourmet eat-in kitchen.

OFFERED AT US$3,750,000
INQUIRIES **Christie's International
Real Estate Westchester and Hudson
Valley**, christiesrehudsonvalley.com
ASSOCIATE David Sanders,
david@sandershomes.com,
+1 845 304 3344
ON THE WEB Search for C59890

LA BEL WORSTELL
FORT MONTGOMERY, ORANGE COUNTY

This eight-bedroom home is
rich with Mediterranean-style
glamour. The 3.8-acre (1.5 ha)
estate boasts majestic river
and mountain views, a large
veranda, a swimming pool,
tennis court, and Zen gardens,
while 14 ft-high (4.3 m-high)
ceilings, moldings, and marble
and Chilean teak floors add
luxurious touches inside.

OFFERED AT US$2,400,000
INQUIRIES **Christie's International
Real Estate Westchester and Hudson
Valley**, christiesrehudsonvalley.com
ASSOCIATE Jacqueline Morales,
jackie@jmhomesteam.com,
+1 845 589 5147
ON THE WEB Search for C59891

MILTON HORSE FARM
WARWICK, ORANGE COUNTY

Located less than an hour
from New York City, this
incredible property extends
over 27.8 acres (11.2 ha), and
is ideal for equestrians. The
farmhouse spans 5,458 sq ft
(507 sq m) and boasts four
bedrooms, four baths, and
a pool, plus there are indoor
and outdoor arenas, a well-
equipped barn, and paddocks.

OFFERED AT US$2,300,000
INQUIRIES **Christie's International
Real Estate Westchester and Hudson
Valley**, christiesrehudsonvalley.com
ASSOCIATE Jacqueline Morales,
jackie@jmhomesteam.com,
+1 845 589 5147
ON THE WEB Search for C59892

NEW YORK, UNITED STATES

NEW YORK, UNITED STATES

REFINED AND TIMELESS

EAST ISLIP, SUFFOLK COUNTY

- Large bulkhead with boatlift
- Close proximity to Fire Island

Rich with Victorian-inspired grandeur, this extraordinary 1.5-acre (0.6 ha) waterfront residence is in an exclusive private community. Sited opposite a wetland preserve, the property affords stunning views of the Great South Bay. Expert craftsmanship is evident throughout, with the grand foyer and its elegant crystal chandeliers providing an impressive welcome.

Coffered ceilings, sconces, and a double-sided fireplace showcase impeccable detailing, while a gourmet kitchen with large island acts as the heart of the home. Elsewhere, five bedrooms, six full baths, and two half baths are a delight. The master suite's double doors add a sense of opulence and reveal a spacious bedroom with a charming balcony and dual baths and closets. Two wonderful fountains and a bluestone patio extend this feeling of regal splendor into the lush garden. A heated pool with a saltwater system is accompanied by a generous spa, adding further luxuries to this immaculately equipped and finished abode.

OFFERED AT US$5,879,000

INQUIRIES **Coach Realtors,** coachrealtors.com

ASSOCIATE Veronica Capuzzo, vcapuzzo@coachrealtors.com, +1 631 252 4157

ON THE WEB Search for C59955

OHIO, UNITED STATES

GORDON HOUSE
MOUNT ADAMS, CINCINNATI

- **Exceptional contemporary design**
- **270-degree city and river views**
- **Two bedrooms and three full baths**

This iconic architectural masterpiece was designed by renowned architects John Meunier and Bertram Berenson in 1983. The landmark property is arguably one of the city's most recognized and revered residences. Sited on the prominent and exclusive southern prow of Mount Adams, the house commands breathtaking views over downtown Cincinnati, the Ohio River, and Kentucky hillsides. A liveable work of art, the open-flowing interiors are highlighted by a double-height semicircular great room with a jaw-dropping floor-to-ceiling window. Further features of note include a well-appointed kitchen, spacious master bedroom awash with natural light, garden-level guest suite boasting stunning views, and an expansive roof deck ideal for alfresco entertaining with the sublime city skyline and frequent fireworks displays as a backdrop. This is a rare opportunity to own one of Cincinnati's most illustrious abodes with incomparable vistas.

OFFERED AT US$1,500,000
INQUIRIES Comey & Shepherd Realtors, comey.com
ASSOCIATE David and Lori Wellinghoff, digs@comey.com, +1 513 403 5520
ON THE WEB Search for C59863

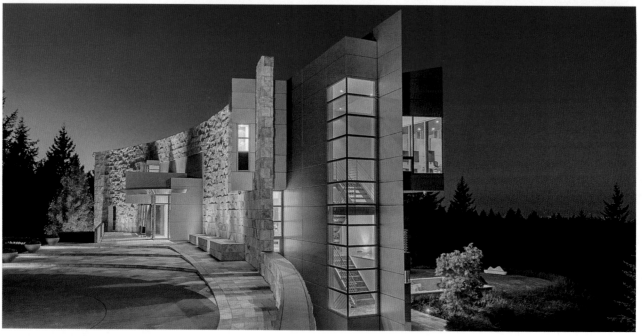

THE LAKOTA RESIDENCE
PORTLAND, MULTNOMAH COUNTY

- **Spectacular views through expansive windows**
- **Four bedrooms plus guesthouse**

Conceived as a fusion of Modernist design and ancient stone, The Lakota Residence is the work of renowned architect Ned Vaivoda. Situated on nearly 10 acres (4 ha) in a coveted location with stunning Cascade mountain vistas, the property is introduced by a tree-lined drive that slowly reveals the unique blend of sleek glass, steel, and concrete interacting with Italian travertine limestone. Inside, light-filled spaces continue this theme, with the natural warmth of wood and stone working in harmony with cantilevered rooms and terraces secured by structural steel. The entry level is dedicated to relaxing, dining, and entertaining, while the lower level is the gateway to expansive patios, a manicured lawn, and a 50 ft (15 m) pool, all secluded by the vast forest reserve that borders the estate. Upstairs hosts four bedrooms, including a spacious master suite with floor-to-ceiling windows affording glorious views, plus an office along a dramatic curved walkway, completing this one-of-a-kind proposition.

OFFERED AT US$8,650,000
INQUIRIES Luxe Christie's International Real Estate, luxecir.com
ASSOCIATE Terry Sprague, terry@luxecir.com, +1 503 459 3987
ON THE WEB Search for C59989

SHANGRI-LA
NARRAGANSETT BAY, BRISTOL HIGHLANDS

- **Seven bedrooms across four residences**
- **Sold in its entirety, or subdivided into lots**

Comprising four residences, this extraordinary 1.8-acre (0.7 ha) waterfront estate is the result of more than 30 years of exquisite landscaping and architectural design. Between them, the primary house, guesthouse, striking glass house, and tea house create a seven-bedroom utopia complete with sandy beach, infinity-edge pool, koi pond, and greenhouses. Expertly conceived outdoor living areas capture the dramatic views of Narragansett Bay, and sculptural plantings provide texture, color, and privacy. Premium details run throughout the estate, from cathedral ceilings and exotic woods in the main home, to the dynamic use of steel and glass in the guesthouse, and the Japanese-style seating on the veranda of the tea house. A historic seaside community with a dock, mooring field, and tennis court, Bristol Highlands is known for its warmth, hospitality, and joie de vivre—a fitting setting for this carefully curated offering, where elegance and natural beauty are elevated to the realm of art.

OFFERED AT US$8,500,000
INQUIRIES **Lila Delman Real Estate**,
liladelman.com; **Christie's
International Real Estate**,
christiesrealestate.com
ASSOCIATES John Hodnett,
john.hodnett@liladelman.com,
+1 401 284 4800; Kathleen Coumou,
kcoumou@christies.com,
+1 212 468 7140
ON THE WEB Search for C59845

RHODE ISLAND, UNITED STATES

COASTAL GRACE

WATCH HILL, WESTERLY

- Nine bedrooms and eight-and-a-half baths
- Beachfront estate in a prime location

Reimagined by award-winning architect Giancarlo Valle, this 1903 classic Shingle-style residence is a magnificent coastal escape that balances an appreciation for contemporary style with comfortable family living. Nearly 10,000 sq ft (929 sq m) of superb interior space encompasses five levels, with a reconfigured modern layout that creates seamless indoor–outdoor appeal. Breathtaking panoramic views of the ocean offer inspiration from vantage points throughout the nine-bedroom house, including the resplendent library. Cooking can be enjoyed in the primary kitchen on a premium La Cornue range, or in the beach-level summer kitchen, with its spectacular backdrop. Beyond the lush plantings, beautiful landscaping, and limestone heated pool of the garden, the estate boasts 160 ft (49 m) of beach frontage and a private cabana from which to take in the tranquil tides. This amazing home was featured in *Architectural Digest* in 2018, and represents a once-in-a-lifetime opportunity.

OFFERED AT US$18,900,000
INQUIRIES **Lila Delman Real Estate**, liladelman.com
ASSOCIATE Lori Joyal, lori.joyal@liladelman.com, +1 401 742 1225
ON THE WEB Search for C59912

MAJESTIC LOG HOME
LANDRUM, GREENVILLE COUNTY

• Gated country club community
• Eight bedrooms and seven full baths
• Hot tub and indoor sports court

Bordering a nature preserve, this tranquil post-and-beam log residence is part of The Cliffs at Glassy, a guarded, gated country club community spanning 3,500 acres (1,416 ha). Equally well suited to serve as a family home or a corporate retreat, the property boasts 12,000 sq ft (1,110 sq m) of sublime living space, including eight bedrooms, seven full baths, and one half bath. The lavish owners' suite is located on the main level, and includes dual full baths and two closets. There is also a chef's kitchen with top-of-the-line appliances, a media room, a vast recreation room, and a sauna for up to 12 people. An indoor half-size court lends itself to basketball and racquetball in all seasons, while the expansive outdoor hot tub and barbecue are great for entertaining. Membership of the country club is available alongside the estate, giving residents access to golf, tennis, hiking, and wellness facilities, as well as dining and clubhouse privileges.

OFFERED AT US$4,500,000
INQUIRIES **BlackStream International Real Estate**, blackstreaminternational.com
ASSOCIATES Holly May, holly@blackstreaminternational.com, +1 864 640 1959, Tim Heatley, tim@blackstreaminternational.com, +1 864 256 3138
ON THE WEB Search for C59935

SOUTH CAROLINA, UNITED STATES

END OF THE ROAD
PAWLEYS ISLAND, GEORGETOWN COUNTY

- **Expansive three-acre (1.2 ha) waterfront estate**
- **Additional independent guesthouse**

Instantly captivating, the antique brick columns and wrought-iron gates of this wonderful home immediately exude opulence. Once a part of Waverly Plantation, which dates back to the 1700s, the original residence underwent a renovation in 2001, when a new construction was added. A perfect balance of formal and casual living spaces has been created, with expansive windows providing panoramic views of the Waccamaw River. State-of-the-art appliances in the stunning kitchen add to the sense of luxury, which is equally evident in the spacious master suite, with spa bath and balcony. A well-kept guesthouse overlooks the spectacular pool and hot tub, which, along with generous porches, decks, and beautiful oversized brick terraces, creates a breathtaking outdoor living space to enjoy amazing sunsets. The historical setting has been thoughtfully preserved, with century-old oaks and cypress trees, southern plantings, and vintage foliage acting as a magnet for a multitude of wildlife.

OFFERED AT US$2,500,000
INQUIRIES **The Lachicotte Company**, pawleysrealestate.com
ASSOCIATE Nancy Siau, nancysiau1@gmail.com, +1 843 450 1835
ON THE WEB Search for C59960

SOUTH CAROLINA, UNITED STATES

CATHERINE JENKINS HOUSE
SOUTH OF BROAD, CHARLESTON

- **Four bedrooms and four-and-a-half baths**
- **Off-street parking for two cars**

A stately home set in a coveted neighborhood, the Catherine Jenkins House combines the characteristic charm of Charleston architecture with customized updates for modern living. Introducing the residence is a spacious foyer that leads to a formal living room and dining room with a beautiful bay window overlooking the piazza. Original chandeliers and hardwood floors infuse the spaces with timeless elegance, while the expansive kitchen, totally renovated in 2008, is a fabulous showpiece that is perfect for entertaining. At the rear of the house, a generous family room invites gatherings, and French doors open to a screened-in veranda with views of the garden. Accommodation comprises four bedrooms, including a master retreat that spans most of the second floor and features an office, a sitting room, and access to the upper-level terrace. This is an uncommon opportunity to reside at a premier Charleston address that boasts a stunning combination of historical details and modern-day convenience.

OFFERED AT US$2,500,000
INQUIRIES **William Means Real**
Estate, LLC, charlestonrealestate.com
ASSOCIATE Helen Geer,
helengeer@williammeans.com,
+1 843 224 7767
ON THE WEB Search for C58829

THE PINNACLE OF LUXURY
RED BUD ISLE, AUSTIN

- **Multilevel decks and a pool**
- **Breathtaking views**

Nestled into the hillside just beyond Red Bud Isle, this statement estate is secluded yet remarkably convenient, just minutes from downtown. One of the most striking modern homes in Austin, its splendid exterior features poured-in-place concrete walls and black slate shingles that create a dramatic juxtaposition against the rolling green hills and city vista.

The intuitive floor plan is introduced by a wide mahogany door opening on to a grand reception space—the perfect spot to highlight any art collection. A resplendent flight of stairs leads up to the spectacular living/dining space characterized by floor-to-ceiling windows that overlook the lush landscape and urban skyline views, while the stunning kitchen is on the entry floor and opens to an outdoor dining area. The main-level master suite is a peaceful oasis with an adjacent bath and dressing room. On the lower level, three bedrooms, a library, and a media room all open to the terrace, pool, and garden, completing this outstanding property.

OFFERED AT US$9,500,000
INQUIRIES **Moreland Properties**, moreland.com
ASSOCIATE Eric Moreland, eric@moreland.com, +1 512 480 0844
ON THE WEB Search for C59866

TEXAS, UNITED STATES

RUSTIC PERFECTION
MEMORIAL PARK, HOUSTON

- **Beautifully finished interiors**
- **Five bedrooms and five-and-a-half baths**

Enviably situated in a desirable area, this magnificent property is surrounded by a lush landscape with unobstructed views of the Hogg Bird Sanctuary and River Oaks Golf Course. The masterpiece of rustic luxury boasts stunning cathedral ceilings and natural stone accent walls in the formal living area, while the gourmet kitchen, renovated in 2018, is outfitted with a full Viking stainless-steel appliance package, separate Sub-Zero cabinet-front refrigerator and freezer, beamed ceilings, expansive counter space and storage, and views to the great room. Breathtaking touches are thoughtfully placed throughout the 8,487 sq ft (788 sq m) home, such as a parlor with dual aquariums, a one-of-a-kind home theater, oversized games room, and beautifully appointed guest accommodation. Five en suite bedrooms feature tray ceilings, walk-in closets, and opulent details, completing the impressive residence, which is perfectly equipped for both grand entertaining and tranquil relaxation.

OFFERED AT US$5,390,000
INQUIRIES **Nan and Company Properties**, nanproperties.com
ASSOCIATE Nancy Almodovar, nancy@nanproperties.com, +1 713 963 9554
ON THE WEB Search for C59887

TEXAS, UNITED STATES

LAKESIDE IDYLL
GRAPEVINE LAKE, TARRANT COUNTY

- Superbly designed four-bedroom penthouse
- Resort-style amenities

Gracefully stretching skyward, The Lakeside Tower delivers 16 stories of luxurious abodes with spectacular outlooks over Grapevine Lake. Presenting contemporary living at its finest, this beautiful 4,500 sq ft (418 sq m) penthouse offers four bedrooms and four-and-a-half baths, high ceilings, and a host of designer finishes. An expansive great room with sweeping lake views and vast nesting glass doors opens to an 1,800 sq ft (167 sq m) wraparound balcony with breathtaking water vistas. Striking solid hardwood flooring flows throughout, while an Italian marble master bath plus a stunning gourmet kitchen with Wolf and Sub-Zero appliances, solid wood cabinetry, and an Italian stone center island create the pinnacle of elegance and sophistication. This impressive property comes with use of the Tower's exclusive resort-style amenities such as a 24/7 concierge, valet, wine room, whiskey bar, state-of-the-art gym, and heated lap pool with cabanas, making this a home like no other.

OFFERED AT US$3,853,500
INQUIRIES **Ulterre**, ulterre.com
ASSOCIATE John Giordano, johng@ulterre.com, +1 817 991 1862
ON THE WEB Search for C59847

SUPERIOR HAVEN

EAGLE MOUNTAIN LAKE, FORT WORTH

- Set on 1.2 acres of lakeside beauty
- Expansive veranda and outdoor pool

Nestled in a spectacular location overlooking Eagle Mountain Lake, this gorgeous estate is a most unique offering. Designed around a grand, open-flowing floor plan that provides ample accommodations for guests and encourages large-scale entertaining, the captivating home boasts exceptional finishes and great attention to detail throughout, with rich hardwood flooring, stained wooden beams, and oversized fireplaces. Highlights of the dazzling interior take in a gourmet kitchen with top-of-the-line stainless-steel appliances and exquisite granite countertops, a refined upstairs living room, and four bedroom suites including a master with private outdoor space. Sublime views of the divine surroundings can be enjoyed throughout the home, as well as from the vast veranda with fireplace and from an additional terrace on the second floor. The impressive 1.2-acre (0.48 ha) manicured grounds also deliver a private dock and a sparkling pool, enhancing the appeal of this ultra-desirable lakeside escape.

OFFERED AT US$2,450,000
INQUIRIES **Ulterre**, ulterre.com
ASSOCIATES Eric Walsh, ericw@ulterre.com, +1 817 312 9586, Rick Wegman, rick@ulterre.com, +1 817 584 7033
ON THE WEB Search for C59906

UTAH, UNITED STATES

MOUNTAIN OPULENCE
PARK CITY, SUMMIT COUNTY

- Impeccable upgrades throughout
- Ski-in/ski-out access to Deer Valley Resort

This beautiful four-bedroom, six-bath home is part of The Belles at Empire Pass mountain community, which is characterized by amazing panoramic views and easy ski access to Deer Valley Resort from the Silver Strike Express and the Northside Express chairlifts. The unique residence has undergone significant upgrades over recent years and now includes top-of-the-line audio/visual and security systems. One of the highlights is the custom-made furniture curated by LA-based designer Beth Ann Shepherd of Dressed Design. Every detail has also been considered in the finishes—there are custom paints and wood stains throughout, bespoke wallpaper selected to complement each space, upgraded lighting, outdoor Bromic heaters on both the upper and lower decks, and handcrafted ironwork on the stairwells. This chic property is offered completely furnished, except for the artwork. Boasting every modern comfort, this is a dream proposition in a sought-after mountain location.

OFFERED AT US$4,995,000
INQUIRIES **Windermere Real Estate-Utah**, winutah.com
ASSOCIATE Matthew Sidford, matthew@sidfordrealestate.com, +1 435 962 4544
ON THE WEB Search for C59939

LE FAUCON

MCLEAN, FAIRFAX COUNTY

- **Seven-bedroom resort-like residence**
- **Five acres with carriage house and barn**

Perfectly sited on five tree-lined acres (2 ha), Le Faucon is the ultimate equestrian estate set amid beautiful countryside, close to the Great Falls national park. Masterfully crafted, the property presents grandeur and sumptuous comfort, with the main home featuring an open-flowing design that spans more than 13,000 sq ft (1,200 sq m) and six bedroom suites. Suitable for multi-generational living, four of the suites have their own entrances and there is also a one-bedroom carriage house apartment. An impressive two-story marble foyer and entrance hall are flanked by a formal living room, elegant dining room, and superb library. These grand spaces are complemented by a relaxed two-story family room adjoining the gourmet kitchen. An outdoor spa, large pool, screened gazebo, outdoor kitchen, and tennis court are further desirable highlights. Completing the resort-like estate are a pristine five-stall barn that has an office on its upper level, pastureland, and a fenced paddock.

OFFERED AT US$5,499,000
INQUIRIES **Long & Foster Real Estate, Inc**, longandfoster.com
ASSOCIATE Dianne Van Volkenburg, dianne@longandfoster.com, +1 703 757 3222
ON THE WEB Search for C59920

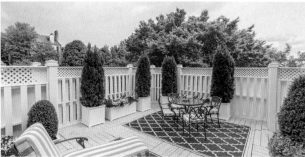

FEDERAL-STYLE GRANDEUR

WEST VILLAGE, GEORGETOWN

- **Five-bedroom home spanning five floors**
- **Period details paired with modern luxury**

This is a stylish, spacious, and sophisticated Federal-style home in a prestigious location. It comprises more than 7,000 sq ft (650 sq m) of elegant living space over five magnificent floors. A wide and welcoming entrance foyer on the reception level boasts sweeping ceilings, majestic crown moldings, and gleaming wooden floors. The double parlor on this floor features smart fireplaces with Egyptian marble mantels. Superb formal staircases and a convenient elevator provide access to the other levels, which deliver five bedrooms, six full baths, and three half baths. The sumptuous master suite has dual baths and walk-in closets, plus an inviting deck with ample room for dining and relaxing. Professionally designed gardens showcase a delightful ornamental fish pond, while four garages and two additional parking bays complete the exterior space. This notable, 200-year-old residence is one of the most beautiful historical houses in the area, fully updated for luxury modern living.

OFFERED AT US$6,500,000

INQUIRIES Long & Foster Real Estate, Inc., longandfoster.com

ASSOCIATE Margaret Heimbold, margaret.heimbold @longandfoster.com, +1 202 812 2750

ON THE WEB Search for C59921

STYLE AND CRAFTSMANSHIP
JACKSON, TETON COUNTY

- Offered completely furnished
- Spectacular surroundings

Located in an idyllic setting, steps from Snake River and Martin Creek, this quintessential contemporary mountain home in the Snake River Sporting Club is the epitome of style, craftsmanship, and sophistication. Designed to disappear into the beautiful landscape of wildflowers and native grasses, the residence's exterior is an exquisite combination of barn wood, limestone, and copper details. Interior highlights encompass wide-plank, French-oak hardwood floors, waterfall quartz countertops, walnut motorized cabinetry, custom leaded-crystal light fixtures, and an array of gorgeous furnishings. A smart gourmet kitchen with electronic cabinets and a built-in Miele touch-screen coffee system makes entertaining and cooking a dream. The great room boasts a wood-burning fireplace and folding doors that open out to the stone patio with a gas firepit and spectacular views of the verdant national forest surrounding the property—the ideal way to enjoy this enviable mountain spot.

OFFERED AT Price upon request
INQUIRIES **Jackson Hole Real Estate Associates, LLC**, jhrea.com
ASSOCIATE Graham-Faupel-Mendenhall, gfm@jhrea.com, +1 307 690 0812
ON THE WEB Search for C59422

HARMONIOUS DESIGN
JACKSON, TETON COUNTY

- Four bedrooms and seven baths
- Impressive spaces and details throughout
- Completion in autumn 2020

The dramatic architecture and exquisite design make an impact at first sight in this impressive mountain home. Understated elegance runs throughout the 5,803 sq ft (539 sq m) residence, which is distinguished by its natural materials and expansive spaces arranged over four floors. Ideal for entertaining, the living area takes in a striking great room and kitchen on the second level, with lofty 20 ft-high (6 m-high) cathedral ceilings and 16 ft (5 m) windows that flood the rooms with natural light. A lower level includes two en suite guest bedrooms, plus a media room with wine cellar, while the second and third floors feature awe-inspiring master suites with beautiful views of the courtyard. An office and garage complete the package. Immaculately designed throughout, this property evokes a sense of serenity and harmony unrivaled in the heart of Jackson Hole, just steps away from the dining, culture, and nightlife of downtown, and outdoor recreation at Snow King Mountain.

OFFERED AT Price upon request
INQUIRIES **Jackson Hole Real Estate Associates, LLC**, jhrea.com
ASSOCIATE Graham-Faupel-Mendenhall, gfm@jhrea.com, +1 307 690 0812
ON THE WEB Search for C59901

WYOMING, UNITED STATES

JEWELLERY - INVITATION TO CONSIGN

As the market leader in this category for 25 consecutive years, Christie's is renowned for selling the finest coloured stones, diamonds, natural pearls and signed jewellery around the world.

To learn more or to schedule a complimentary and confidential valuation, please do not hesitate to contact us.

RUBY AND DIAMOND 'MYSTERY SET'
EARRINGS, VAN CLEEF & ARPELS
Sold for: CHF 200,000
Magnificent Jewels,
Geneva, 15 May 2019

Geneva

CONTACT
Jean-Marc Lunel
jlunel@christies.com
+41 (0) 22 319 1730

Hong Kong

CONTACT
Vickie Sek
vsek@christies.com
+852 2978 9922

London

CONTACT
Keith Penton
kpenton@christies.com
+44 (0) 20 7389 2526

Los Angeles

CONTACT
Peggy Gottlieb
pgottlieb@christies.com
+1 310 385 2665

Monaco

CONTACT
Nancy Dotta
ndotta@christies.com
+377 97 97 11 00

New York

CONTACT
Daphne Lingon
dlingon@christies.com
+1 212 636 2300

Paris

CONTACT
Violane d'Astorg
vdastorg@christies.com
+33 1 40 76 85 81

Shanghai

CONTACT
Caroline Liang
cliang@christies.com
+86 212 226 1520

CHRISTIE'S

ISLANDS & OCEANS

Pages 237-246

ANTIGUA & BARBUDA

PENTHOUSE NUMBER ONE
ST JOHN'S, ANTIGUA

- **Designed to maximize the stunning views**
- **Outstanding attention to detail**

With a spectacular outlook over Falmouth Bay to the hills beyond, this stylish property is both spacious and luxurious, while incorporating the latest developments in energy-efficient technology. High-end living with the wow factor is on offer here, with soaring ceilings and an impressive curved-glass and stainless-steel illuminated staircase. The chef's kitchen and interior living and dining areas all extend out on to a generous, west-facing veranda that offers the perfect place to watch the sun setting over the bay. A sumptuous grand master suite on the upper floor has a relaxing, open-plan feel with a dressing area and ample closets, and its own terrace boasting stunning views over the water to the hills beyond. There are also two spacious guest bedrooms with their own baths on the upper floor. Outside, the secluded sun deck delivers a sunken seating area, a vast shaded pergola, a swimming pool, an outdoor shower, and a gas barbecue area, all surrounded by herb planters and beautiful landscaping.

OFFERED AT US$2,950,000
INQUIRIES One Caribbean Estates Antigua,
onecaribbeanestatesantigua.com
ASSOCIATE Justin White, jwhite @onecaribbeanestatesantigua.com, +1 268 725 4059
ON THE WEB Search for C59962

BAHAMAS

VICTORIA POINT CAY
MANGROVE CAY, ANDROS

- **Two rustic properties on a secluded island**
- **Wooded trails, sandy beaches, and a helipad**

Covering almost 10 acres (4 ha), Victoria Point Cay lies within the South Bight of Andros and comes with every amenity to enjoy the freedom of island life amid abundant wildlife and nature. Fresh water, electricity, telephone, and internet services are all connected to the estate's two houses via underwater piping and cable from the mainland. These traditional properties include a two-bedroom main residence and a three-bedroom guesthouse. Highlights of the primary home encompass a fantastic living room with fireplace and an elegant library, while, adjacent to this, an office/utility room boasts a lookout tower, complete with 360-degree views of the ocean. The guest quarters have an outdoor bath plus a large wraparound covered porch, perfect for enjoying the sublime surroundings. Diving, snorkeling, and fishing are afforded by the cay's location, and a floating dock can accommodate small vessels. Pairing home comforts with tropical island luxury, Victoria Point Cay is a magical offering.

OFFERED AT US$3,100,000
INQUIRIES **H.G. Christie Ltd**,
hgchristie.com
ASSOCIATES Cara Christie,
cara@hgchristie.com,
John Christie, john@hgchristie.com,
+1 242 322 1041
ON THE WEB Search for C59961

BARBADOS

ATELIER HOUSE
CARLTON, SAINT JAMES

- **Contemporary four-bedroom retreat**
- **Stunning infinity-edge pool**

This stylish, contemporary 5,608 sq ft (521 sq m) villa sits on a ridge with magnificent views across a mahogany tree-filled gully and beyond to the Caribbean Sea. The panoramas can be enjoyed from the large infinity-edge pool, or from the extensive terrace and living areas, which include a double-height indoor space to maximize the vistas. Surrounded by half an acre (0.2 ha) of beautifully lush gardens with indigenous palms, lilies, bougainvillea, and flowering shrubs, Atelier House exudes a level of finesse, elegance, and design rarely available in Barbados. Inside, one of the many highlights is the upstairs master suite, which boasts a glazed balcony, as well as a covered terrace, providing ideal spots for enjoying the gorgeous surroundings. Elsewhere, three spacious guest bedrooms are located on the first floor: one with its own bath and outdoor shower. This sophisticated, light-filled residence delivers luxurious indoor–outdoor living perfect for making the most of the Barbadian climate.

OFFERED AT US$3,950,000
INQUIRIES **One Caribbean Estates,**
onecaribbeanestates.com
ASSOCIATE Chris Parra,
info@onecaribbeanestates.com,
+1 246 620 4105
ON THE WEB Search for C59872

BERMUDA

CAPER COLLIS
TUCKER'S TOWN, HAMILTON PARISH

- **Six bedrooms and seven full baths**
- **Pool, pool house, and studio apartment**
- **Breathtaking water and ocean views**

Poised atop a 2.38-acre (0.96 ha) promontory, near one of the Mid Ocean Club's charming pink sand beaches, Caper Collis is one of Bermuda's most intriguing luxury residences. A meandering drive leads to this 6,000 sq ft (557 sq m) single-level home with an extensive swimming pool and versatile pool house. The striking entrance with its traditional cedar front door opens to a travertine-tiled foyer. Beyond is the generous living room with spectacular cherry floors and three sets of French doors to a long terrace with sublime Atlantic views, which can also be enjoyed from the study, dining room, and kitchen. The family room leads to a vast covered terrace with panoramic vistas over Mangrove Lake to the Mid Ocean Club golf course. There is a master suite, two guest suites, and three further suites, plus a studio apartment adjoining the pool house, which is ideal for staff or further guest accommodation.

OFFERED AT Price upon request
INQUIRIES **Sinclair Realty Ltd**,
sinclairrealty.com
ASSOCIATE Karin H Sinclair,
estates@sinclairrealty.com,
+1 441 296 0278
ON THE WEB Search for C59963

MANGO MANOR

SHANNON ESTATE, TORTOLA

• **Gorgeous grounds with hot tub and pool**
• **Expansive decks for entertaining**

Impressing with 25,000 sq ft (2,323 sq m) of living space across the magnificent main house, guesthouse, caretaker's cottage, and fabulous decks, this incredible compound represents an unparalleled island retreat. Sited on a lush hillside, the property enjoys the spectacular scenery of nearby beaches and turquoise waters. Characterized by plantation-style furnishings and expansive rooms, the residence offers the perfect luxury family escape. A majestic living space with vaulted ceilings and large glass doors that offer up breathtaking ocean views, a billiards room, a fully equipped kitchen, and spacious en suite bedrooms create an interior sanctuary. Outside, 10,000 sq ft (929 sq m) of covered decks provide ample room for alfresco entertaining and serene relaxation, while the grounds also take in a hot tub and gorgeous infinity-edge pool with slide. Guests are well catered for with a two-bedroom self-contained guesthouse and a one-bedroom cottage, and a two-car garage completes the sublime estate.

OFFERED AT US$6,900,000

INQUIRIES **Smiths Gore BVI Limited**, smithsgore.com

ASSOCIATE Lucienne Smith, lucienne.smith@smithsgore.com, +1 284 543 1028

ON THE WEB Search for C59986

CARIBBEAN DREAM
YACHT CLUB, GRAND CAYMAN

• **Bright living spaces with designer features**
• **Private dock on a picturesque canal**

Situated in one of Grand Cayman's most distinguished neighborhoods, this private canalfront estate has beautifully landscaped grounds lined with lush palms and indigenous flora. The two-story residence is filled with chic features thanks to acclaimed interior designers Design Studio, complemented by extraordinary mosaic tiles and built-in hardwood cabinetry by Ironshore Contractors. Serene canal and garden views abound from the floor-to-ceiling windows throughout. The inviting dining area, gym, and home theater make this abode ideal for entertaining. Secluded on the second floor, the spacious master suite has an en suite bath with a grand soaking tub, plus a private terrace with space to lounge while overlooking the glittering canal. Outside, the patio is a great spot for soaking up the Caribbean sun, while the Zen garden is perfect for reading or yoga, and the large infinity-edge swimming pool is a dream. A grilling cabana with alfresco dining space and 60-ft (18 m) dock complete the offer.

OFFERED AT US$6,950,000
INQUIRIES **Provenance Properties Cayman Islands**,
provenanceproperties.com
ASSOCIATE Ruth Gustafsson,
ruth.gustafsson
@provenanceproperties.com,
+1 345 526 3633
Member of CIREBA MLS#: 408806
ON THE WEB Search for C59275

THE RESIDENCES AT SEAFIRE
SEVEN MILE BEACH, GRAND CAYMAN

• **Stunning ocean views**
• **Access to Kimpton Seafire Resort + Spa**

Perfectly positioned on 12 spectacular acres, (4.9 ha) with blissfully open grounds on Seven Mile Beach, this superb three-bedroom condo sits within a luxury 62-unit complex. The lush landscaping, cascading pools, and turquoise waters of the Caribbean provide the perfect backdrop for this nearly 3,000 sq ft (279 sq m) property. A spacious terrace, which can be converted into additional interior space via its folding glass NanaWalls, invites the outdoors in, while an ample master suite enjoys its own terrace, as well as a walk-in closet. Two further bedrooms look out over the beautiful canals of the North Sound and feature en suite baths. The kitchen is a delight, with a Miele gas stove and Sub-Zero appliances, alongside marble countertops and gorgeous custom cabinets. Another wonderful addition is access to the fabulous amenities of the adjacent Kimpton Seafire Resort + Spa, while owners can also choose to place their residence in an optional rental program managed by the hotel team.

OFFERED AT US$3,400,000
INQUIRIES **Provenance Properties Cayman Islands**,
provenanceproperties.com
ASSOCIATE Fleur Coleman,
fleur.coleman
@provenanceproperties.com,
+1 345 325 7204
ON THE WEB Search for C59938

CAYMAN ISLANDS

MOUNTAIN SPLENDOR

CABEZAS, FAJARDO

- **Swimming pool, Jacuzzi, and wet bar**
- **Spectacular ocean views**
- **Eight bedrooms and seven full baths**

Nestled amid 2.47 acres (1 ha), this superb property—adjacent to the golf course of El Conquistador, A Waldorf Astoria Resort—consists of a pair of two-level residential structures, totaling 7,616 sq ft (707 sq m), set against a dramatic ocean and mountain backdrop. These pristine surroundings help to create an ambience of rare magnificence. The main structure houses the living quarters, which include several dining and recreation areas, as well as a high-end kitchen, while the second building contains eight bedrooms, seven baths, and two kitchenettes. There is also an array of entertainment facilities, from a gazebo with its own wet bar to a swimming pool, Jacuzzi, and gym. Additional amenities include a three-car garage; plentiful storage space; expansive balconies and terraces, which are perfect for enjoying the sunsets; separate manager's quarters; a power generator to run the entire complex; and a helipad.

OFFERED AT US$1,600,000

INQUIRIES **Trillion Realty Group, Inc.**, trillionrealtygroup.com

ASSOCIATES Letty Brunet, letty@trillionrealtygroup.com, +1 787 378 7386, Molly Assad, molly@trillionrealtygroup.com, +1 787 642 3205

ON THE WEB Search for C57311

ISLANDS & OCEANS

SAINT BARTHÉLEMY

VILLA SBS
LORIENT BAY

- **Extensive grounds with ocean views**
- **Ideal for stylish entertaining**

Located in Lorient bay, this beachfront home is designed for an exceptional indoor–outdoor lifestyle. Decorated in a high-end contemporary style, the luxurious residence offers stunning views of the ocean and the neighboring islands. The main living area consists of a fully equipped kitchen with breakfast bar, interior dining space for eight people, and a comfortable living room. This opens to a covered terrace set in the sand that has a mirror-effect pool and a Jacuzzi, as well as a lounge and second dining area, making it ideal for entertaining. Shaded by royal palm trees for added privacy, the terrace, with its large sun deck, leads directly down to the sea. Four exquisite bedrooms with en suite baths and walk-in showers are located on either side of the terrace, all facing the ocean. A fifth bedroom with en suite bath, kitchen, and terrace is nestled in the rear garden. This exceptional villa, with easy access to the beach, is beautifully finished with the latest top-of-the-range fixtures and fittings.

OFFERED AT US$15,500,000
INQUIRIES **Sibarth Real Estate**, sibarthrealestate.com
ASSOCIATE Zarek Honneysett, zarek@sibarthrealestate.com, +590 590 29 88 91
ON THE WEB Search for C59853

christiesrealestate.com

POINT HOUSE
PARROT CAY

- **Premier island setting with ocean views**
- **Access to first-class resort amenities**

A refined beachfront estate that spans more than 7,000 sq ft (650 sq m), Point House is one of just 12 exquisite properties on the exclusive private island of Parrot Cay. Occupying a lush, covetable site alongside a nature reserve, with glorious beach views, the majestic home was designed by renowned architect Cheong Yew Kuan. Beautifully finished ceilings soar to 30 ft (9 m), vast windows are framed in white oak, and glass doors bathe interiors in sunlight. Four bedrooms boast indulgences such as outdoor showers and opulent en suite baths, while a secluded fifth bedroom nestles amid botanic gardens. Stone floors and natural wood finishes encapsulate the pared-back aesthetic that defines this inviting residence, where an open-plan living and dining room opens to a covered terrace and pool. Everything about the villa encourages a seamless indoor–outdoor lifestyle and casually elegant gatherings; it has an exceptional blend of comfort and warmth, shoreline elegance and sophistication.

OFFERED AT US$15,000,000
INQUIRIES Regency,
theturksandcaicos.com;
Christie's International Real Estate,
christiesrealestate.com
ASSOCIATES Robert Greenwood,
robert@tcibrokers.com,
+1 649 432 7653, Hazel Rush,
hazel@tcibrokers.com,
+1 649 232 0999; Rick Moeser,
rmoeser@christies.com,
+1 561 805 7327
ON THE WEB Search for C59885

An American Place: The Barney A. Ebsworth Collection
STEFAN HIRSCH (1899-1964)
Excavation
signed with initials and dated 'SH 1926' (on the license plate at lower right)
oil on canvas
35½ x 45 in. (90.2 x 114.3 cm.)
Painted in 1926.
Price Realized: $399,000
American Art, New York, 22 May 2019

AMERICAN ART

New York, 20 November 2019

We are now accepting consignments for our upcoming
auctions. Please do not hesitate to contact us to find out
when a specialist will be in your area.

CONTACT
William Haydock
whaydock@christies.com
+1 212 636 2140

CHRISTIE'S

**FINE & RARE WINES: THE 40 YEARS
JUBILEE OF ALPINA FINE WINE**

Geneva, 10 November 2019

VIEWING
8-9 November
Quai des Bergues 33
1201 Genève, Switzerland

CONTACT
Edwin Vos
evos@christies.com
+31 613 17 0974

CHRISTIE'S

SOUTH & CENTRAL AMERICA

Pages 249-253

FRENCH-STYLE MANSION
BELGRANO, BUENOS AIRES

- Gorgeous gardens with pool
- Convenient elevator access to every floor

Situated behind secure gates, this impressive, French-style property comprises 12,917 sq ft (1,200 sq m) of covered living space across three stories. Ideal for both grand entertaining and intimate family living, the interior blends large, open rooms with more cozy retreats. The first floor incorporates a living room, primary kitchen, dining area, and home office, along with a light-filled conservatory. On the second level, three en suite bedrooms, each with its own dressing room, join a master suite with double dressing room, hydromassage in the bath, and a delightful balcony. A living room and family room complete this floor. The third story and its private office can be accessed by the stairs or via the convenient elevator that serves every level. Further highlights include a spacious basement, and a staff apartment on the third floor. Outside, the spectacular grounds boast a dazzling pool and a *quincho*—a space dedicated to barbecues and hosting gatherings —plus a games area/gym, and an events hall.

OFFERED AT Price upon request
INQUIRIES **ReMind Group SA**, remind.com.ar
ASSOCIATE Carolina Dumais, carolina@remind.com.ar, +5411 4352 4325
ON THE WEB Search for C59984

BRAZIL

LUXURY RETREAT
FAZENDA BOA VISTA, PORTO FELIZ

- **Community with golf, tennis, and spa facilities**
- **Beautiful surroundings**
- **Ideal for indoor–outdoor entertaining**

With charming Provence-style architecture and panoramic views of amazing sunsets, this incredible property is located in front of the Arnold Palmer-designed golf course in the exclusive gated community of Fazenda Boa Vista. The grand 1.24-acre (0.5 ha) estate includes a residence of 12,917 sq ft (1,200 sq m) with spacious living and dining rooms, an office, home theater, gym, wine cellar, and six bedroom suites—all fully furnished. Outside, an expansive terrace with barbecue area and dining space is ideal for alfresco entertaining overlooking the beautiful gardens and surrounding landscape, while a sports court and swimming pool provide fabulous leisure options, and a six-car garage delivers convenience for guests. The community of Fazenda Boa Vista is located just 80 miles away from São Paulo and offers impressive facilities including the golf course, tennis courts, an equestrian center, a spa, and a number of trails.

OFFERED AT Price upon request
INQUIRIES **Axpe Imóveis Especiais**, axpe.com.br
ASSOCIATE Luiza Cazarin, luiza.cazarin@axpe.com.br, +55 11 3074 3600
ON THE WEB Search for C59907

CHILE

LAGO PIRIHUEICO HAVEN
VALDIVIA, LOS RIOS

- **Unrivaled natural beauty**
- **Bursting with development potential**

With a name that in the indigenous language means Lagoon of Snow, this spectacular tract of land, with its clear, glittering waters, is a glorious offering like no other. Located on one of the most exclusive lakes in Chile, the acreage provides supreme tranquility, with the surrounding land beautifully preserved. Engulfed by native forest, the parcel includes more than 2.5 miles (4 km) of north-facing sandy beach, as well as the stunning waters of a 934-acre (378 ha) lagoon, plus two flowing rivers. Opportunities abound, with the outer areas accessible by road, but much of the space remaining completely unspoiled and ideal for a number of development options. An exclusive residential community would be well suited to the peaceful beach area, and the rivers and lagoon are ideal for fishing and small-scale watersports. The sheer splendor of the natural beauty also encourages preservation or the farming of sustainable produce. This is a breathtaking proposition filled with potential.

OFFERED AT Price upon request
INQUIRIES Bórquez & Asociados Limitada, byas.cl
ASSOCIATE Maria José Bórquez Yunge, contacto@byas.cl, +56 229 536 992
ON THE WEB Search for C59852

CASA COLUMBO
LOS SUEÑOS, PUNTARENAS

- **11 bedrooms, 14 full baths, and 4 half baths**
- **Private registered heliport**

This elegant villa is a sumptuous and supremely tranquil retreat from city life. Stretching across 27,000 sq ft (2,508 sq m), the mansion sits amid spectacular rainforest, atop the highest hill in a luxurious beachfront resort. With three bays, a world-class marina, and Herradura beach nearby, there is no limit to the splendid vistas. Stunning front doors and a palatial two-story grand foyer with domed ceiling set a majestic precedent for the interiors, which incorporate Honduran mahogany, floor-to-ceiling custom doors and windows, coffered ceilings, and custom cabinetry throughout. An elevator serves all floors from basement to heliport. The gourmet kitchen has a vast center island and breakfast space, while a lavish master suite includes a sitting area, balcony, dual baths, and closets. Outside, further beauty awaits, with a gorgeous pool and pool bar plus an array of fabulous sitting and dining spaces. The serene tropical setting elevates this fine home above its peers, as the crown jewel of Los Sueños.

OFFERED AT US$10,600,000
INQUIRIES **Plantación Properties**, costaricarealestate.online
ASSOCIATE Robert F Davey, bob@ppcire.com, +877 661 2060
ON THE WEB Search for C59983

SIGNATURE STYLE

*Our exclusive global affiliates are pleased to offer
a selection of distinctive Signature Properties.
Discover more at* **christiesrealestate.com/signature**

MODERN CAPE DUTCH
CAPE TOWN, SOUTH AFRICA

Sited in the foothills of Constantiaberg, this elegant Cape Dutch villa showcases sublime mountain views. Six en suite bedrooms, open-plan reception rooms, a modern kitchen, and a park-like garden with designer pool make the residence perfect for indoor–outdoor living. Close to some of the country's top wine estates, as well as restaurants, golf courses, and shopping, this home has it all. ZAR 24m
Greeff Properties Marie Durr, marie@greeff.co.za, +27 83 269 8608, Ashley Barnes, ashley@greeff.co.za, +27 83 261 3996, Cheryl Teubes, cheryl@greeff.co.za, +27 82 457 9980

COMFORT AND STYLE
CAPE TOWN, SOUTH AFRICA

This magnificent home has been designed to embrace breathtaking vineyard and mountain views. Fabulous living spaces flow easily out to a sensational deck with sparkling solar-heated pool. Five lavish bedroom suites include a self-contained apartment, while a resplendent sunken library, a gym, a wine cellar with tasting room, and a games room combine to make entertaining a breeze. ZAR 38m
Greeff Properties Ashley Barnes, ashley@greeff.co.za, +27 83 261 3996, Cheryl Teubes, cheryl@greeff.co.za, +27 82 457 9980, Marie Durr, marie@greeff.co.za, +27 83 269 8608

LAKESIDE PANORAMA
FEUSISBERG, ZURICH, SWITZERLAND

From its unrivaled position enveloped by meadows and lush forests, this fantastic property incorporates walls of glass that capture awe-inspiring views across Lake Zurich and the Glarus Alps. Its open-plan layout includes a dining area, designer kitchen, and sumptuous lounge anchored by a firepit. This opens to a grand terrace with an infinity-edge pool that seems to flow into the lake below. A wine cellar, spa, gym, and Jacuzzi ensure a lifestyle beyond compare. Price upon request
Wüst und Wüst AG Stefanie Oechslin, stefanie.oechslin@wuw.ch, +41 44 388 58 40

MOUNTAIN GRANDEUR
ASPEN, CO, USA

Remodeled in 2010, this stunning modern mountain home offers the quintessential Aspen experience on six acres (2.4 ha), with glorious views of the majestic peaks. Seven bedrooms, five fireplaces, a sauna, a hot tub, and a workout area are interior highlights, while the grounds are an equestrian paradise. Completely private, yet only 10 minutes from downtown Aspen, included are a barn, workshop, riding arena, and trail access. $9.5m
Christie's International Real Estate
Michelle Sullivan, michelle@christiesaspenre.com, +1 970 366 0168

SNOW DRIFT RANCH
PLACERVILLE, CO, USA

Dominating the pinnacle of the most photogenic spot in Colorado is Snow Drift Ranch. Spanning 10,000 square feet (929 sq m) on a 138-acre (56 ha) lot, this mountain trophy home has been meticulously designed by the seller to be a self-reliant fortress on top of the Dallas Divide, conveniently sited near Telluride and Ridgway, and close to airports, the famous hot springs, and some of the best skiing in the entire West. $12.5m
Telluride Real Estate Corp.
Robert Stenhammer, robert@telluriderealestates.com, +1 970 708 7771

SERENE ELEGANCE
ESSEX, CT, USA

An amazing English-style conservatory with walls of glass and a cathedral ceiling is the centerpiece of this sophisticated early 19th-century home known as The Elijah Worthington Residence. Thoughtfully updated, the living areas feature original fireplaces, while the master suite benefits from a sublime bath. Outside is no less splendid, with magnificent gardens, a heated pool, an English cutting house, and winter views that stretch from North Cove to the Connecticut River and the hills of Lyme. $1.999m
Page Taft Chip Frost, cfrost@pagetaft.com, +1 860 388 7848

MOUNTAIN MASTERPIECE
FAIRVIEW, NC, USA

This modern mountain sanctuary was designed to welcome the outdoors in. Retractable screens and cascading doors blend the outdoor kitchen, living area, and firepit with the indoor living spaces, all overlooking a picturesque wooded lot. A sumptuous owners' suite with fireplace, vaulted ceiling, and wine bar, plus two further bedroom suites provide plenty of accommodation, while a clubroom with wet bar and a sunken media room offer a range of entertainment options. $1.3m
Ivester Jackson BlackStream
Britt Allen, britt@ijbproperties.com, +1 828 450 8166

CASTLE LADYHAWKE
TUCKASEGEE, NC, USA

Set among the pristine backdrop of the Blue Ridge mountains and just 20 minutes from Cashiers, this is a fairy-tale castle situated on 16 acres (6.5 ha). Every detail of the four-bedroom, five-bath home is dramatic, from soaring ceilings to vast decks and terraces. Enhanced by lavish grounds and sweeping views, the superb manor includes an expansive great room, an intricate three-level staircase, bedroom suites with spa-like baths, a home office, a pub, and a three-car garage. $3m
Ivester Jackson BlackStream
Damian Hall, dh@damianhallgroup.com, +1 864 561 7942

TRADITIONAL BEAUTY
CHARLOTTE, NC, USA

Located in a sought-after neighborhood, this 10,800 sq ft (1,003 sq m) manor is situated on 4.7 gorgeous acres (1.9 ha). Glorious grounds include formal gardens, walking trails, a pavilion with fireplace, a saltwater pool, and sports courts. Inside, the four-bedroom home boasts intricate millwork, a chef's kitchen with butler's pantry, a wine cellar, a library, and a grand owners' retreat with a terrace. $4.5m
Ivester Jackson Distinctive Properties
Tracy Davis, tracy@ivesterjackson.com, +1 704 779 9750, Reed Jackson, reed@ivesterjackson.com, +1 704 713 3623

FAIRWINDS CASTLE
LANDRUM, SC, USA

Sporting all the hallmarks of an English country estate, from a resplendent gated entrance and verdant pastures to a stately stone tower, this is a magical residence. Fourteen rooms across three floors are filled with bespoke items such as stained-glass doors, floor-to-ceiling bookcases, and antique chandeliers, while gorgeous grounds provide a pool, a firepit, a pond, a two-stall barn, and horse paddocks. The home is also just minutes from Tryon International Equestrian Center. $1.75m
BlackStream International Real Estate
Damian Hall, dh@damianhallgroup.com, +1 864 561 7942

RELAXING FAMILY HOME
CORSICANA, TX, USA

Remodeled in 2000, this wonderful estate comprises 7.5 fenced acres (3 ha). A four-bedroom primary home offers multiple living areas including a formal dining room with soaring ceilings, an intimate den, and a glorious master suite with ample walk-in closets. This is joined by a three-car garage with an art room, a workspace, and plenty of storage. The grounds are a recreational delight, taking in a raised deck, limestone pergola, koi pond, waterfall, playground, and zip line, as well as a barn. Price upon request
Ulterre Pete Coulborn, petec@ulterre.com, +1 214 668 6031

GET IN TOUCH

Contact details for the exclusive affiliates of Christie's International Real Estate

Europe & Africa

AUSTRIA

Avantgarde Properties
Vienna, Austria
+43 1 890 55 33
avantgardeproperties.com
Elisabeth Karoly-Thomas

**Stiller & Hohla
Immobilientreuhänder
GmbH**
Salzburg, Austria
+43 662 6585 110
stiller-hohla.at
Franz Stiller, Leo Hohla

CZECH REPUBLIC

Svoboda & Williams
Prague, Czech Republic
+420 257 328 281
svoboda-williams.com
Cyril Dejanovski

FRANCE

Agence Clerc Immobilier
Veyrier du Lac, France
+33 4 50 64 88 88
agence-clerc.com
Benoit Clerc

Belles Demeures de France
(see also Daniel Féau Conseil
Immobilier)

Corse Prestige Immobilier
Corsica, France
+33 4 95 25 90 41
corseprestige.com
Emmanuel Castellani

Côte Ouest Immobilier
Saint-Jean-de-Luz, France
+33 5 59 26 82 60
coteouest-immobilier.com
Nicolas Descamps

**Daniel Féau Conseil
Immobilier**
Paris, France
+33 1 40 08 10 04
feau-immobilier.fr
Charles-Marie Jottras,
Marie-Hélène Lundgreen

David Bilder Real Estate
La Baule Escoublac, France
+33 6 60 10 07 00
davidbilder.com
David Bilder

**Maxwell-Baynes
Real Estate**
Merignas, France
+33 5 57 84 08 82
maxwellbaynes.com
Karin Maxwell,
Michael Baynes

**Michaël Zingraf
Real Estate**
Cannes, France
+33 4 93 39 77 77
michaelzingraf.com
Michaël Zingraf

Poncet & Poncet
Occitante, France
+33 4 67 02 03 31
poncet-poncet.com
Patrick Poncet

GREECE

**Ploumis Sotiropoulos
Real Estate**
Athens, Greece
+30 210 364 3112
ploumis-sotiropoulos.gr
Yannis Ploumis

IRELAND

Sherry FitzGerald
Dublin, Ireland
+353 1 237 6394
sherryfitz.ie
Michael Grehan

ITALY

**Agenzia Romolini
Immobiliare Srl**
Anghiari, Arezzo, Italy
+39 0575 788948
romolini.com
Riccardo Romolini

Immobilsarda Srl
Porto Cervo, Sardinia, Italy
+39 0789 909000
immobilsarda.com
Julia Bracco

La Commerciale Srl
Rome, Italy
+39 06 32 00 613
lacommercialerealty.com
Maurizio Pezzetta

MONACO

**Hammer Draff
Great Properties**
Monte Carlo, Monaco
+377 97 97 63 33
hammerdraff.com
Monica de Champfleury

MOROCCO

**Kensington Luxury
Properties**
Marrakech, Morocco
+212 5 24 422 229
kensingtonmorocco.com
Alex Peto

NETHERLANDS

Residence 365 BV
Amsterdam, The Netherlands
+31 20 2610 430
r365.nl
Leslie DT de Ruiter

PORTUGAL

LUXIMO'S
Porto, Portugal
+351 961 696 319
Algarve, Portugal
+351 289 035 465
luximos.pt
Ricardo Costa

This exceptional Paris apartment has lovely gardens with views of the Eiffel Tower. On the market with Belles Demeures de France (Daniel Féau Conseil Immobilier); see page 96 for more details.

Porta da Frente, Lda
Lisbon, Portugal
+351 214 826 830
portadafrente.com
Rafael Ascenso

SLOVAKIA

Svoboda & Williams
(see Czech Republic)

SOUTH AFRICA

Greeff Properties
Cape Town, South Africa
+27 21 763 4120
greeff.co.za
Mike Greeff

SPAIN

Costa Del Sol 365
Marbella, Spain
+31 6 4535 7522
costadelsol365.es
Hans Veenhuijsen

Estela Exclusive Homes
Ibiza, Spain
+34 971 931 562
estelaexclusivehomes.com
Sandra Tejero Estévez

Rimontgó
Valencia, Spain
+34 96 350 4444
rimontgo.com
Antonio Ribes Bas,
José Ribes Bas

SWEDEN

Residence Fastighetsmäkleri
Stockholm, Sweden
+46 8 662 6800
residence.se
Lars Fogelklou

SWITZERLAND

SPG Finest Properties
Geneva, Switzerland
+41 22 707 46 60
spgfinestproperties.ch
Thierry Barbier-Mueller

**Wetag Consulting
Immobiliare SA**
Locarno, Switzerland
+41 91 751 31 06
wetag.ch
Ueli F Schnorf

Wüst und Wüst AG
Zurich, Switzerland
+41 44 388 58 73
wuw.ch
Herbert Wüst

UNITED KINGDOM

Strutt & Parker
London, England
+44 20 7484 8105
struttandparker.com
Rory Field

Asia Pacific

AUSTRALIA

Ken Jacobs
Double Bay, New South Wales,
Australia
+61 2 9328 1422
kenjacobs.com.au
Ken Jacobs

Prestige Homes of Victoria
Melbourne, Victoria, Australia
+61 4 2578 7979
prestigehomes.com.au
Sean Cussell

HONG KONG

**Landscope Christie's
International Real Estate**
Hong Kong SAR
+852 2866 0022
landscope-christies.com
KS Koh

JAPAN

Japan Capital Realty, Inc.
Tokyo, Japan
+81 3 5404 8570
jcrealty.jp
Sonny Saito

MALDIVES

Dutch Docklands Maldives
Malé, Maldives
+960 333 666 4
dutchdocklands.com
Jasper Mulder

TAIWAN

Jubon Assets Management
Taipei City, Taiwan
+886 2 3765 5678
realty.com.tw
Michael Liu

Nestled in parkland, this period property in a village on the Swiss side of Lake Geneva has been completely renovated. On the market with SPG Finest Properties; see page 119 for more details.

THAILAND

**Richmont's Luxury
Real Estate**
Bangkok, Thailand
+66 2 670 8288
richmonts.com
Tim Skevington

North America

CANADA

BRITISH COLUMBIA

Faith Wilson Group
Vancouver, British Columbia,
Canada
+1 604 224 5277
faithwilsongroup.com
Faith Wilson, Keith Harfield

Newport Realty
Victoria, British Columbia,
Canada
+1 250 385 2033
newportrealty.com
Jack Petrie, John Hayes

ONTARIO

**Chestnut Park Real Estate
Limited, Brokerage**
Toronto, Ontario, Canada
+1 416 925 9191
chestnutpark.com
Chris Kapches

**Marilyn Wilson Dream
Properties Inc. Brokerage**
Ottawa, Ontario, Canada
+1 613 842 5000
dreamproperties.com
Marilyn Wilson

**Niagara-on-the-Lake
Realty, Ltd**
Niagara-on-the-Lake,
Ontario, Canada
+1 905 468 3205
notlrealty.com, notlrealty.ca
Christopher Bowron,
Thomas Elltoft

QUEBEC

Profusion Realty Inc.
Westmount, Quebec, Canada
+1 514 935 3337
profusion.global
Louise Rémillard

MEXICO

BAJA CALIFORNIA SUR

2Seas Los Cabos
Los Cabos, Baja California Sur,
Mexico
+52 624 105 2547
2seasloscabos.com
Ramiro Palenque Bullrich

GUANAJUATO

CDR San Miguel
San Miguel de Allende, Mexico
+52 415 154 8804
cdrsanmiguel.com
Ann Dolan, Jim Dolan,
Nancy Howze

MEXICO CITY

LUXMX Bienes Raices
Mexico City, Mexico
+52 415 103 3374
luxmx.com
Joseph W Lown

NEUVO LEON

**Gerencia RED
Grupo Inmobiliario**
Garza García, Mexico
+52 818 363 1212
gerenciared.com
Gerardo Gutiérrez

UNITED STATES

ARIZONA

Walt Danley Realty
Paradise Valley, Arizona
+1 480 991 2050
waltdanley.com
Walt Danley

CALIFORNIA

Dilbeck Estates
La Cañada Flintridge, California
+1 877 345 2325
dilbeckestates.com
Mark Dilbeck

First Team Real Estate
Newport Beach, California
+1 949 759 5747
firstteam.com
Michael Mahon

HK Lane Real Estate, Inc.
Palm Desert, California
+1 760 834 7500
hklane.com
Harvey Katofsky, Eden Naigle

**Oliver Luxury Real
Estate Tahoe**
Lake Tahoe, California
+1 530 581 1100
oliverlux.com
Michael Oliver
(see also Nevada)

Richardson Properties, Inc.
San Luis Obispo, California
+1 805 781 6040
richardsonproperties.com
Charles H Richardson,
Chris Richardson

Strand Hill Properties
Palos Verdes, California
+1 310 541 6566
Manhattan Beach, California
+1 310 545 0707
strandhill.com
Chris Richardson

Village Properties Realtors
Montecito, California
+1 805 969 8900
villagesite.com
Renée Grubb

Willis Allen Real Estate
San Diego, California
+1 877 515 7443
willisallen.com
Ashley McEvers

COLORADO

**Christie's International
Real Estate, Aspen**
Aspen, Colorado
+1 970 658 8222
christiesrealestate.com
Alex Jansen, Laren Jansen

Telluride Real Estate Corp.
Telluride, Colorado
+1 970 728 3111
telluriderealestatecorp.com
TD Smith

CONNECTICUT

Neumann Real Estate
Ridgefield, Connecticut
+1 203 438 0455
neumannrealestate.com
Russ Neumann, Chip
Neumann, Bob Neumann,
Shaylene Neumann,
Jeff Neumann

Randall Realtors
Mystic, Connecticut
+1 860 572 9099
randallrealtors.com
H Douglas Randall,
Michael Schlott

DELAWARE

**Long & Foster Real
Estate, Inc.**
(see also Virginia)

FLORIDA

**American Caribbean
Real Estate**
Islamorada, Florida
+1 305 664 4966
americancaribbean.com
Joy Martin

**Coastal Properties Group
International, LLC**
Clearwater Beach, Florida
+1 727 424 4978
jansencoastal.com
Alex Jansen, Laren Jansen

Set in one of Mexico
City's few green spaces,
this home perfectly
blends modern and
classical design. On
the market with LUXMX
Bienes Raices; see page
154 for more details.

Highlights of this six-bedroom Montana home include incredible living spaces and stunning mountain views. On the market with PureWest Real Estate; see page 198 for more details.

Fenton & Lang
Jupiter Island, Florida
+1 772 546 2381
fentonandlang.com
Adrian Reed, Lia Reed

Illustrated Properties Real Estate, Inc.
Palm Beach Gardens, Florida
+1 561 282 5276
ipre.com
Mike Pappas

Michael Saunders & Company
Sarasota, Florida
+1 941 552 5212
michaelsaunders.com
Michael Saunders

Premier Estate Properties, Inc.
Boca Raton, Florida
+1 561 394 7700
premierestateproperties.com
Joseph G Liguori

Palm Beach, Florida
+1 561 655 5505
premierestateproperties.com
Carmen D'Angelo

Regal Real Estate
Orlando, Florida
+1 407 749 0700
regalrealtyorlando.com
Chris Christensen

William Raveis Real Estate
Naples, Florida
+1 239 213 0800
naplesluxuryhomes.com
Bill Raveis

GEORGIA

Harry Norman, Realtors
Atlanta, Georgia
+1 404 504 7300
harrynorman.com
Jenni Bonura

Seabolt Brokers, LLC
Savannah, Georgia
+1 912 233 6609
seaboltbrokers.com
Elaine Seabolt

HAWAII

Hawaii Life Real Estate Brokers
Big Island, Hawaii
+1 800 370 3848
Kauai, Hawaii
+1 800 370 3848
Maui County, Hawaii
+1 800 370 3848
Oahu, Hawaii
+1 800 370 3848
hawaiilife.com
Matt Beall

IDAHO

Jackson Hole Real Estate Associates, LLC
(see also Wyoming)

Sun Valley Real Estate LLC
Ketchum, Idaho
+1 208 726 6000
sunvalleyrealestate.com
Suzanne Williams,
Tom Drougas, Brad DuFur

KENTUCKY

Comey & Shepherd Realtors
(see also Ohio)

MAINE

LandVest, Inc.
(see also Massachusetts)

MARYLAND

Long & Foster Real Estate, Inc.
(see also Virginia)

MASSACHUSETTS

Great Point Properties, Inc.
Nantucket, Massachusetts
+1 508 228 2266
greatpointproperties.com
Bill Liddle, Greg Mckechnie,
Edward Sanford

LandVest, Inc.
Boston, Massachusetts
+1 617 723 1800
landvest.com
Ruth Kennedy Sudduth
(see also Maine, New Hampshire, New York, Rhode Island, and Vermont)

Pine Acres Realty
Chatham, Massachusetts
+1 508 945 1186
pineacresrealty.com
Lori Fanning-Smith,
Chris Rhinesmith

MICHIGAN

Hall & Hunter Realtors
Birmingham, Michigan
+1 248 644 3500
hallandhunter.com
Dennis J Wolf, Brad Wolf

North Harbor Real Estate
Petoskey, Michigan
+1 231 881 9400
lakecharlevoix.com
Jeff Wellman, Lora Higdon,
Jay Higdon

MONTANA

PureWest Real Estate
Bozeman, Montana
+1 406 586 9418
Whitefish, Montana
+1 406 862 4900
purewestrealestate.com
Sean Averill,
Dale Crosby Newman,
Scott Strellnauer

NEVADA

Oliver Luxury Real Estate
Reno, Nevada
+1 775 236 1500
oliverlux.com
Michael Oliver

Elite Homes US, LLC
Las Vegas, Nevada
+1 702 787 8061
elitehomes.us
Lisa Song Sutton, Cathey Kuo

NEW HAMPSHIRE

LandVest, Inc.
(see Massachusetts)

NEW JERSEY

Christie's International Real Estate, Northern New Jersey
Ramsey, New Jersey
+1 201 934 0607
christiesrennj.com
Ilija Pavlovic, Sonja Cullaro

Gloria Nilson & Co. Real Estate
Princeton, New Jersey
+1 609 921 2600
Rumson, New Jersey
+1 732 530 2800
glorianilson.com
Patricia Bell

Long & Foster Real Estate, Inc.
(see also Virginia)

Special Properties, a Division of Brook Hollow Group, Inc.
Saddle River, New Jersey
+1 201 934 7111
specialproperties.com
Vicki Gaily

NEW MEXICO

Barker Realty Inc.
Santa Fe, New Mexico
+1 505 982 9836
santaferealestate.com
Lisa and David Barker

NEW YORK

Christie's International Real Estate Group
New York, New York
+1 877 399 0177
christiesrealestate.com
Kathleen Coumou

Christie's International Real Estate Westchester and Hudson Valley
New City, New York
+1 201 345 7780
christiesrehudsonvalley.com
Sonja Cullaro

Coach Realtors
Northport, New York
+1 631 757 4000
coachrealtors.com
Lawrence P Finn,
Georgianna F Finn

LandVest, Inc.
(see Massachusetts)

NORTH CAROLINA

Ivester Jackson BlackStream
Asheville, North Carolina
+1 828 367 9001
ivesterjacksonblackstream.com
Reed Jackson, Lori Ivester
Jackson, Ford Elliott

Ivester Jackson Distinctive Properties
Cornelius, North Carolina
+1 704 655 0586
ivesterjackson.com
Reed Jackson,
Lori Ivester Jackson
(see also South Carolina)

Looking out over the water from its unique hilltop location, Caper Collis is a classically elegant Bermuda estate. On the market with Sinclair Realty Ltd; see pages 241 for more details.

OHIO

Comey & Shepherd Realtors
Cincinnati, Ohio
+1 513 561 5800
comey.com
Scott Nelson
(see Kentucky)

OREGON

**Luxe Christie's
International Real Estate**
Lake Oswego, Oregon
Portland, Oregon
Bend, Oregon
+1 503 389 2112
luxecir.com
Terry R Sprague,
Kendra Ratcliff,
Vince Cortese
(see also Washington)

PENNSYLVANIA

**Long & Foster Real
Estate, Inc.**
(see also Virginia)

RHODE ISLAND

LandVest, Inc.
(see Massachusetts)

Lila Delman Real Estate
Newport, Rhode Island
+1 401 789 6666
liladelman.com
John Hodnett

SOUTH CAROLINA

**BlackStream International
Real Estate**
Greenville, South Carolina
+1 864 901 4078
blackstreaminternational.com
Ford Elliott, Carlos Salgado

**Ivester Jackson
Distinctive Properties**
(see North Carolina)

The Lachicotte Company
Pawleys Island, South Carolina
+1 843 237 2094
lachicotte.com
Christy Whitlock

**William Means Real
Estate, LLC**
Charleston, South Carolina
+1 843 577 6651
charlestonrealestate.com
Helen L Geer

TEXAS

Moreland Properties
Austin, Texas
+1 512 480 0848
moreland.com
Emily Moreland

**Nan and Company
Properties**
Houston, Texas
+1 713 714 6454
nanproperties.com
Nancy Almodovar

Ulterre
Dallas, Texas
+1 817 336 5172
Fort Worth, Texas
+1 817 336 5172
gwwrealestate.com
Rick Wegman, John Giordano,
Eric Walsh

UTAH

**Windermere Real
Estate-Utah**
Park City, Utah
+1 435 649 3000
winutah.com
Grady Kohler

VERMONT

LandVest, Inc.
(see Massachusetts)

VIRGINIA

**Long & Foster Real
Estate, Inc.**
Chantilly, Virginia
+1 800 237 8800
longandfoster.com
Duane Giglia, Barry Redler
(see also Delaware, Maryland,
New Jersey, Pennsylvania,
Washington, DC, and
West Virginia)

WASHINGTON

**Luxe Christie's
International Real Estate**
(see Oregon)

WASHINGTON, DC

**Long & Foster Real
Estate, Inc.**
(see Virginia)

WEST VIRGINIA

**Long & Foster Real
Estate, Inc.**
(see Virginia)

WYOMING

**Jackson Hole Real
Estate Associates, LLC**
Jackson, Wyoming
+1 888 733 6060
jhreassociates.com
Julie Faupel (see Idaho)

Islands & Oceans

ANTIGUA & BARBUDA

**One Caribbean
Estates Antigua**
Saint John's, Antigua
+268 736 7910
onecaribbeanestatesantigua.com
Craig Ryan

ARUBA

Residence 365 BV
Amsterdam, The Netherlands
+31 10 22 508 22
r365.nl
Leslie DT de Ruiter
(see also Bonaire, Curaçao,
Saba, and Sint Eustatius)

BAHAMAS

H.G. Christie Ltd
Nassau, Bahamas
+1 242 322 1041
hgchristie.com
William McPherson Christie,
John Christie

BARBADOS

**One Caribbean
Estates Limited**
Saint James, Barbados
+246 620 4105
onecaribbeanestates.com
Chris Parra

BERMUDA

Sinclair Realty Ltd
Hamilton, Bermuda
+1 441 296 0278
sinclairrealty.com
Karin and John M Sinclair

BONAIRE

Residence 365 BV
(see Aruba)

BRITISH VIRGIN
ISLANDS

Smiths Gore BVI Limited
Tortola, British Virgin Islands
+1 284 494 2446
smithsgore.com
Edward Childs, Lucienne Smith

CAYMAN ISLANDS

**Provenance Properties
Cayman Islands**
Grand Cayman, Cayman Islands
+1 345 640 3500
provenanceproperties.com
Jackie Doak

CURACAO

Residence 365 BV
(see Aruba)

PUERTO RICO

Trillion Realty Group, Inc.
San Juan, Puerto Rico
+1 787 925 2520
trillionrealtygroup.com
Leticia Brunet González,
Ana Rosa González Brunet

SABA

Residence 365 BV
(see Aruba)

SAINT BARTHELEMY

Sibarth Real Estate
Saint Barthélemy,
French West Indies
+590 590 29 88 91
sibarthrealestate.com
Christian Wattiau

SINT EUSTATIUS

Residence 365 BV
(see Aruba)

TURKS & CAICOS
ISLANDS

Regency
Providenciales,
Turks & Caicos Islands
+1 649 941 4100
theturksandcaicos.com
Walter Gardner,
Robert Greenwood

US VIRGIN ISLANDS

John Foster Real Estate
Saint Thomas, US Virgin Islands
+1 340 775 9000
usvi-realestate.com
Nick Bailey, Peter Briggs

Central
America

COSTA RICA

Plantación Properties
Playa Flamingo, Costa Rica
+506 2654 4004
plantacionproperties.com
Robert Davey

South America

ARGENTINA

ReMind Group SA
Buenos Aires, Argentina
+54 11 4325 4325
Bariloche, Argentina
+54 294 444 8530
remind.com.ar
Fernanda Canals, Agustín Larco

BRAZIL

Axpe Imóveis Especiais
São Paulo, Brazil
+55 11 3074 3600
axpe.com.br
José Eduardo Cazarin

CHILE

**Bórquez & Asociados
Limitada**
Santiago, Chile
+56 2 2953 6992
byas.cl
María José Bórquez
(see also Peru)

PERU

**Bórquez & Asociados
Limitada**
Lima, Peru
+51 1 711 3919
byas.pe
María José Bórquez, Maria
Fernanda Herrera (see Chile)

Christie's
International
Real Estate

NORTHEAST
UNITED STATES
& CANADA

Kathleen Coumou
Executive Director,
Northeast Region
20 Rockefeller Plaza
New York
New York 10020, USA
+1 212 468 7140
kcoumou@christies.com

WESTERN
UNITED STATES
& CANADA

Zackary Wright
Executive Director,
Western Region
336 North Camden Drive
Beverly Hills
California 90210, USA
+1 310 385 2690
zwright@christies.com

SOUTHEAST,
SOUTHWEST,
CENTRAL
& MOUNTAIN
UNITED STATES,
CARIBBEAN &
LATIN AMERICA

Rick Moeser
Executive Director,
Southeast, Southwest,
Central & Mountain Region,
Caribbean & Latin America
313 1/2 Worth Avenue,
Suite 4B
Palm Beach
Florida 33480, USA
+1 561 805 7327
rmoeser@christies.com

EUROPE, MIDDLE
EAST, INDIA & AFRICA

Helena De Forton
Head of Regional Operations,
EMEA
Monique Ghosh
Global Head of Referrals
8 King Street
St James's
London SW1Y 6QT, UK
+44 20 7389 2299
mghosh@christies.com
+44 20 3824 1951
emea@christiesrealestate.com

RUSSIA

Olga Tsoy
Romanov pereulok 2/6-13
Moscow, 125009
Russia
+7 495 937 6364
otsoy@christies.com

ASIA PACIFIC

Zackary Wright
Executive Director,
Asia Pacific
22nd Floor, Alexandra House
18 Chater Road
Central, Hong Kong
+852 2978 6788
zwright@christies.com

A two-story grand foyer with domed ceiling and Honduran mahogany detail introduces this 11-bedroom retreat in Costa Rica. On the market with Plantación Properties; see page 253 for more details.

Blue heaven: Signed and dated 'Yves Klein 59' on the reverse, *Rélief éponge bleu (RE 51)* realized £7,657,250/$11,952,967 at a Post-War and Contemporary Art auction at Christie's London in 2012.

Design icon

INTERNATIONAL KLEIN BLUE

Yves Klein, 1960

In 1947 a young Yves Klein (1928–62) was on a beach in the South of France with two friends. To pass the time the trio decided to divide up the world among themselves. One chose to take the land and its riches, the other the air. Klein chose the sky and its infinity. He then, so the story goes, laid back and gazed at the sky, declaring: "The blue sky is my first artwork." Years later a particular shade of blue would cement the artist's place in history. International Klein Blue (IKB) was developed by Klein in partnership with Parisian art paint supplier Edouard Adam. The instantly recognizable shade owes its uniqueness to a matte, synthetic resin binder in which its ultramarine pigment is suspended. Klein registered the formula in 1960, going on to use IKB in paintings and on human models. IKB provides the background for the entirety of Derek Jarman's final film, 1993's *Blue*. Jarman chose it to represent the loss of his sight, which was developing a blue tinge as a result of AIDS-related complications.